MW00914834

YELLOWSTONE & GRAND TETON
NATIONAL PARKS TRAVEL GUIDE
2024

Exploring Nature's Spectacles and Thrilling Outdoor
Adventures in the Heart of the American West in 3 Days

NICHOLAS INGRAM

COPYRIGHT

Copyright © 2023 **Nicholas Ingram**

This publication is protected by copyright. No part of it may be reproduced, distributed, or transmitted in any form or by any means, including photocopying, recording, or electronic or mechanical methods, without the prior written permission of the publisher. Brief quotations embodied in critical reviews and certain other noncommercial uses permitted by copyright law are an exception.

This book serves as an informational guide and reference only. The author and publisher are not liable for any damages or expenses incurred by individuals or entities based on the information contained in this book. Readers are responsible for their own safety and security while traveling.

While every effort has been made to ensure the accuracy and currency of the information in this book at the time of publication, the author and publisher do not assume responsibility for any errors or omissions that may occur or for subsequent changes.

In the heart of untamed landscapes,

where nature's majesty unfolds,

Yellowstone and Grand Teton,

where wild stories are told.

Mountains soaring high,

rivers rushing with fervent might,

These parks preserve wonders,

captivating day and night.

CONTENTS

Copyright

INTRODUCTION   1

Yellowstone National Park   2

Grand Teton National Park   4

CHAPTER 1: PLANNING YOUR TRIP   7

Why You Should Visit Yellowstone & Grand Teton National Parks   8

Best Time to Visit   9

Summer Packing List   10

Winter Packing List   11

Cost of Visiting Yellowstone & grand teton national park   12

How to Get There   16

Park Regulations and Permits   17

CHAPTER 2: THE GATEWAY TOWNS TO YELLOWSTONE AND GRAND TETON NATIONAL PARKS   19

Jackson Hole, WY   20

West Yellowstone, MT   23

Bozeman, MT   26

Cody, WY   29

Gardiner, MT   31

Big Sky, MT   33

Other Nearby Towns   35

CHAPTER 3: WHAT TO DO & SEE IN YELLOWSTONE — 42

Top 10 Attractions — 43

Geothermal Marvels — 56

Yellowstone Lakes — 59

Yellowstone Valleys — 60

Wildlife Watching — 63

Hiking — 66

Scenic Drives — 74

Boating, Kayaking & Fishing — 79

Camping — 81

Photography — 86

Ranger-Led Programs — 89

Historic Sites and Museums — 92

CHAPTER 4: WHAT TO SEE & DO AT THE GRAND TETON NATIONAL PARK — 104

Top 10 Must-See Features of Grand Teton National Park — 105

Top 10 Activities in Grand Teton National Park — 125

Outdoor Adventures — 128

Hiking: 10 Best Hikes & Trails in Grand Teton National Park — 129

Climbing and Mountaineering — 133

Wildlife Viewing — 135

Rafting, Boating and Kayaking — 137

Camping — 140

Biking — 143

Photography — 146

Scenic Drives   148

Fishing   150

Visitor Centers & Interpretive Programs   154

CHAPTER 5: ITINERARY   158

Adjustable 3-days Itinerary For Visiting   159
Yellowstone & Grand Teton national parks

Best 2-Day Yellowstone National Park Itinerary   162

3-Day Grand Teton Itinerary for HIKING   164
Enthusiasts

CHAPTER 6: FOOD & RESTAURANTS   168

6 Local Food to Enjoy In Yellowstone & Grand   169
Teton

Top 10 Yellowstone Restaurants & Bars   170

Top 10 Restaurants in Grand Teton National Park   173

Top 5 Restaurants In Jackson Hole, Wyoming   176

Top 5 Restaurants In Cody, Wyoming   178

YOUR FEEDBACK   180

CHAPTER 7: WHERE TO STAY IN YELLOWSTONE   181
AND GRAND TETON

10 Budget-Friendly Places To Stay In Yellowstone   182
National Park

7 Budget-Friiendly Places To Stay In Grand Teton   186
National Park

Best Campground to Stay In Grand Teton   189

CHAPTER 8: GETTING AROUND YELLOWSTONE &   190
GRAND TETON

NATIONAL PARKS

Getting Around Yellowstone   192

Yellowstone Snowcoach Transportation   193

Getting Around Grand Teton   194

CHAPTER 9: NIGHTLIFE, FESIVALS AND EVENTS   195

Nightlife in Yellowstone & Grand Teton   196

Festivals in Yellowstone & Grand Teton   197

Events in Yellowstone & Grand Teton   201

CHAPTER 10: EXPLORING YELLOWSTONE AND   202
GRANDTETON FOR CHILDREN

CHAPTER 11: PRACTICAL INFORMATION   204

Packing List   205

Shopping & Souvenirs   207

Safety Tips and Guidelines   208

Useful Contacts   210

Useful Resources   211

MAP   212

MAP 1: Old Faithful Trail Map   213

MAP 2: Old Faithful Area Trail Map   214

MAP 3: Norris Geyser Basin Trail Map   215

MAP 4: Mammoth Hot Springs Trail Map   216

MAP 5: West Thumb Geyser Basin Trail Map   217

Map 6: Grand Canyon of the Yellowstone Trail Map   218

MAP 7: Fountain Paint Pot trail map   219

CONCLUSION   220

OTHER BOOKS BY THIS AUTHOR   221

ABOUT THE AUTHOR   223

YOUR FEEDBACK   225

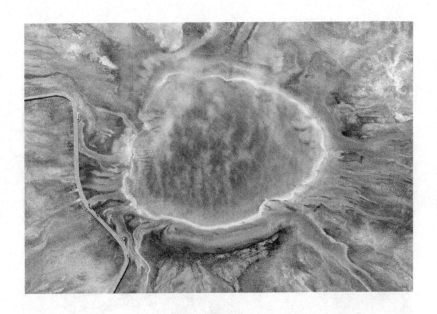

INTRODUCTION

- Overview of the Yellowstone National Park
- Overview of the Grand Teton National Park

YELLOWSTONE NATIONAL PARK

Grand Canyon at Yellowstone National Park - Photo By Brocken Inaglor

Yellowstone National Park, established in 1872, holds the distinction of being not only the first national park in the United States but also the world. Located primarily in the state of Wyoming, with parts extending into Montana and Idaho, Yellowstone spans an area of over 2 million acres, showcasing a mesmerizing landscape of geothermal wonders, majestic mountains, pristine lakes, and diverse wildlife. The park is renowned for its impressive geothermal features, including geysers, hot springs, mud pots, and fumaroles. The most famous of these is Old Faithful, a geyser known for its predictable eruptions, shooting boiling water and steam into the air at regular intervals. Yellowstone sits atop one of the world's largest active volcanic systems, which fuels these geothermal phenomena and contributes to the park's unique geological character.

Beyond its geothermal wonders, Yellowstone boasts a rich biodiversity. The park is home to a wide variety of wildlife, including iconic species such as grizzly bears, gray wolves, bison, elk, and bighorn sheep. You have the opportunity to observe these animals in their natural habitats, making Yellowstone a premier destination for wildlife enthusiasts and nature lovers alike. Yellowstone's landscape is also characterized by its stunning natural features. Towering peaks, deep canyons, lush forests, and pristine rivers and waterfalls contribute to the park's breathtaking scenery. Yellowstone Lake, one of the largest high-elevation lakes in North America, adds to the park's allure with its serene beauty and opportunities for recreation such as fishing, boating, and kayaking.

Y ou can explore its wonders through a network of roads and trails that traverse the park's diverse terrain. Whether hiking through backcountry wilderness, marveling at colorful hot springs, or simply taking in the grandeur of the landscape, there are endless opportunities for adventure and discovery within Yellowstone. In addition to its natural splendor, Yellowstone holds cultural significance as well. The park is home to archaeological sites that provide insight into the lives of Native American tribes who have inhabited the region for thousands of years. Historic structures such as the Old Faithful Inn and the Roosevelt Arch also offer glimpses into Yellowstone's past and the early days of conservation in the United States.

Yellowstone National Park stands as a testament to the beauty and power of nature, drawing millions of visitors each year to experience its wonders and to be inspired by its timeless landscapes.

GRAND TETON NATIONAL PARK

Disappointment Peak (center), hiding Grand Teton, with Middle Teton and Garnet Canyon on the left and Mt. Owen and Glacier Gulch on the right - Photo From Wikimedia by user Acroterion

N estled in northwestern Wyoming, adjacent to Yellowstone National Park, lies the spectacular Grand Teton National Park. Encompassing approximately 310,000 acres of pristine wilderness, the park is celebrated for its towering mountain peaks, pristine alpine lakes, abundant wildlife, and diverse ecosystems, making it a haven for outdoor enthusiasts and nature lovers. At the heart of the park are the Teton Range, a dramatic mountain range characterized by jagged peaks that soar abruptly from the valley floor. The Grand Teton, the tallest peak in the range at 13,770 feet (4,197 meters), commands attention with its sheer granite walls, challenging climbers & captivating photographers alike. Surrounding the Grand Teton are a series of other impressive peaks, including Mount Owen, Middle Teton, and South Teton, collectively forming one of the most iconic mountain landscapes in North America.

Grand Teton National Park is not only renowned for its breathtaking scenery but also for its abundant wildlife. You have the opportunity to encounter a diverse array of animals, including elk, moose, bison, bighorn sheep, black bears, grizzly bears, and elusive mountain lions. The park's varied habitats, from alpine meadows to dense forests and riparian areas, provide vital refuge for these species, contributing to the park's ecological richness. The park's numerous lakes, such as Jenny Lake, Jackson Lake, and Leigh Lake, offer stunning reflections of the surrounding mountains and provide opportunities for fishing, boating, kayaking, and swimming. Hiking trails wind through forests, meadows, and alpine terrain, leading adventurers to hidden waterfalls, scenic overlooks, and secluded backcountry campsites. Popular trails include the Cascade Canyon Trail, Paintbrush Canyon Trail, & the iconic hike to Hidden Falls & Inspiration Point. In addition to its natural beauty, Grand Teton National Park holds cultural significance as well. The park is home to historic sites, including Mormon Row, where you can explore remnants of early homesteading in the region, and the Chapel of the Transfiguration, a rustic chapel with stunning views of the Teton Range. The Grand Teton National Park offers a wealth of opportunities for exploration, adventure, and contemplation amidst some of the most awe-inspiring landscapes in the American West. Whether marveling at towering peaks, encountering wildlife in their natural habitat, or simply soaking in the serenity of alpine lakes, visitors to Grand Teton are sure to be captivated by its timeless beauty and boundless wilderness.

The proximity of Yellowstone National Park and Grand Teton National Park allows you to explore both parks in a single trip, often referred to as the "Yellowstone and Grand Teton Loop." This loop provides a distinctive chance to encounter the varied terrains and extraordinary natural marvels of both parks, encompassing geothermal attractions and majestic mountain summits, displaying the abundant and diverse splendor of the American West.

CHAPTER 1: PLANNING YOUR TRIP

- Why You Should Visit Yellow Stone & Grand Teton National Parks
- Cost of Visiting Yellowstone
- Best Time to Visit
- How to Get There
- Accommodation Options
- Park Regulations and Permits

WHY YOU SHOULD VISIT YELLOWSTONE & GRAND TETON NATIONAL PARKS

1. UNIQUE GEOTHERMAL FEATURES: Yellowstone National Park boasts the world's largest concentration of geysers, including the famous Old Faithful, along with hot springs, mud pots, and colorful geothermal pools, providing visitors with a mesmerizing display of natural wonders and geological phenomena.

2. BREATHTAKING SCENERY: Grand Teton National Park offers stunning panoramic views of the jagged Teton Range, pristine alpine lakes, and lush valleys, making it a paradise for outdoor enthusiasts, photographers, and nature lovers alike.

3. ABUNDANT WILDLIFE VIEWING: Both parks are home to a diverse array of wildlife, including iconic species such as grizzly bears, wolves, bison, elk, moose, and bald eagles, providing unparalleled opportunities for wildlife enthusiasts to observe these majestic creatures in their natural habitats.

4. OUTDOOR RECREATION: From hiking and camping to fishing, boating, and wildlife watching, Yellowstone and Grand Teton National Parks offer a wide range of outdoor recreational activities for visitors of all ages and skill levels, ensuring an unforgettable adventure amidst breathtaking natural beauty.

5. RICH CULTURAL AND HISTORICAL SIGNIFICANCE: These parks are not only renowned for their natural beauty but also for their rich cultural and historical significance, with evidence of Native American presence and early exploration by fur trappers and pioneers, providing visitors with a deeper understanding of the region's heritage.

BEST TIME TO VISIT

The best time to visit Yellowstone and Grand Teton National Parks depends on what activities you're interested in and your tolerance for crowds and weather.

1. SUMMER (JUNE-AUGUST): This is the peak season with warm weather, open roads, and all facilities operational. However, it's also the busiest time, so expect large crowds & heavy traffic, especially around popular attractions like Old Faithful. This is the best time for hiking, wildlife viewing, and enjoying the full range of activities both parks offer.

2. SPRING (APRIL-MAY) AND FALL (SEPTEMBER-OCTOBER): These shoulder seasons offer fewer crowds, cooler temperatures, and beautiful scenery. Spring brings blooming wildflowers and newborn wildlife, while fall offers vibrant foliage. Some facilities may start to close towards the end of the fall season, but many attractions remain open. These seasons are excellent for hiking and wildlife viewing, but be prepared for variable weather, including potential snowfall, especially in the early spring and late fall.

3. WINTER (NOVEMBER-MARCH): Winter transforms both parks into a winter wonderland. While many roads and facilities close during this time, visitors can enjoy unique activities like cross-country skiing, snowshoeing, and snowmobiling (in designated areas). The parks are much quieter in winter, offering a more serene experience, but be prepared for cold temperatures and limited services.

The best time to visit depends on your preferences for weather, crowds, and activities. If you prefer fewer people and don't mind colder temperatures, the shoulder seasons and winter can provide a more intimate experience with nature. However, if you want to take advantage of all the park's amenities and activities, summer might be the best choice despite the crowds.

SUMMER PACKING LIST

WHAT TO WEAR SUMMER

T-shirt: Pack one for each day. | *Hiking socks:* Opt for non-cotton trekking socks for comfort. | *Hiking pants:* Convertible pants are versatile for changing weather | *Underwear:* Bring one pair for each day or opt for ExOfficio for convenience. | *Swimwear:* Essential for hot springs or a dip in Lake Yellowstone. | *Water shoes:* Sturdy athletic sandals are ideal for various activities. | *Hiking boots or walking shoes:* Oboz offers quality options for all-day comfort. | *Sun hat:* Protect yourself from the intense sun with a broad-brimmed hat. | *Sunglasses:* Polarized lenses are essential for glare reduction. | *Midweight layer:* A fleece layer is handy for cooler mornings and evenings.

WHAT TO PACK IN SUMMER

Food: Buy groceries ahead of time to save money and time. | *Refillable water bottle:* Metal bottles are eco-friendly and durable. | *Binoculars or spotting scope:* Enhance wildlife watching experiences. | *Bug spray:* Essential for protection against mosquitoes. | *Bear spray:* Important for safety in bear country. | *Sunscreen:* Protect your skin from the sun's rays. | *Cooler and picnic basket:* Ideal for outdoor meals and snacks. | *Camp chair:* Handy for wildlife watching or relaxing by the river | *Camera lenses/Phone battery:* Capture memories with a fully charged device. | *Quick dry travel towel:* Useful for water activities or hot springs. | *Multi-tool:* Be prepared for various situations with a versatile tool. | *First aid kit:* Essential for minor injuries and illnesses. | *Headlamp:* Handy for nighttime activities or emergencies. | *Plastic bags:* Useful for waste disposal or organizing items. | *Yellowstone National Park map:* Essential for navigation within the park. | *Day pack/backpack:* Carry essentials comfortably during your adventures. | *Child backpack carrier:* Convenient for families with young children.

WINTER PACKING LIST

Accessing Yellowstone in winter requires proper planning. While some northern areas are accessible year-round by car, other parts necessitate over-snow vehicles like snowcoaches or snowmobiles. Snowy roads lead to some of the park's most breathtaking sights, including Old Faithful and the Grand Canyon of the Yellowstone. Hotels and rental accommodations are available throughout the winter in nearby towns like West Yellowstone and Gardiner.

WINTER ESSENTIALS CHECKLIST:

Base Layer: Start with thermal underwear made of silk, wool, or polypropylene. | **Midweight Layer:** Add a fleece or similar layer for insulation and moisture-wicking. | **_Heavy Weight Layer:_** Keep warm with a down jacket or heavy wool sweater. | **_Outer Layer:_** Top it off with a water-resistant snow parka to shield against the elements. | **_Snow Pants:_** Essential for outdoor activities to keep your legs warm and dry. | **_Accessories:_** Include warm gloves or mittens, insulated hats, non-cotton socks, scarves or neck gaiters, and knee-high gaiters to keep snow out of your boots. | **_Footwear:_** Insulated, waterproof snow boots are a must-have. | **_Additional Gear:_** Consider cross-country skis, snowshoes, traction cleats, and hand and toe warmers for outdoor adventures. | **_Other Necessities:_** Bring a swimsuit for hot springs, water shoes, lodgewear, sleepwear, sunglasses, and sunscreen. | **_Equipment:_** Don't forget a camera with extra batteries, a multi-tool, a first aid kit, a headlamp, and a Yellowstone map for navigation. | Prepare for varying temperatures, which can range from below zero to 20°F (-20 to -5°C), with sub-zero temperatures common at night and at higher elevations. Snowfall can be heavy, so be ready for snowy conditions. Dress in layers, opt for moisture-wicking fabrics, and ensure you have proper insulation and waterproof gear for a comfortable and safe Yellowstone winter adventure.

COST OF VISITING YELLOWSTONE & GRAND TETON NATIONAL PARK

To calculate the combined cost of visiting both Yellowstone and Grand Teton National Parks together, we'll need to consider various expenses such as travel, accommodation, food, entertainment, and any additional gear or fees. Let's break it down:

1. TRANSPORTATION: *To Get There:* Flights into nearby airports like Jackson, Wyoming; Idaho Falls, Idaho; or Bozeman, Montana can range from a few hundred dollars. If you're flying into Jackson Hole Airport for Grand Teton, consider flight prices to and from your location. If driving, calculate the cost of gas and potential overnight stays en route. Transportation costs depend on your mode of travel. Calculate the total distance and estimate fuel costs based on your vehicle's fuel efficiency and current fuel prices. Add any additional transportation costs within the parks, such as vehicle entrance fees.

To Get Around: To explore both Grand Teton National Park and Yellowstone, having a private vehicle is essential due to limited public transportation options. Travelers typically spend around $52 and $37 per person per day in In Grand Teton & Yellowstone National Parks respectively on local transportation, encompassing fuel costs and park entrance fees. Private transfer services offer a more luxurious or hassle-free option for exploration in Grand Teton. While private vehicles are necessary in Yellowstone, guided bus tours from nearby resorts offer informative and convenient ways to experience Yellowstone's highlights.

2. ENTRANCE FEES: *Yellowstone National Park* charges entrance fees: $35 for a private, non-commercial vehicle, valid for 7 days. | $20 per person for individuals entering on foot, bicycle, ski, etc. | $70 for an annual pass covering entrance fees for everyone in the vehicle. | *Grand Teton National Park* charges private, non-commercial vehicle - $35; Motorcycle - $30; Individual on foot, bicycle, or noncommercial group - $20 per person. | *TIPS:* If you have plans to visit multiple national parks within a year, it is recommended to purchase the America the Beautiful Pass. This pass grants access to all federally-managed land units, including national parks, national forests, national monuments, and more. Valid for one year from the month of purchase, it offers convenience and cost savings for your national park visits.

3. ACCOMMODATION: Estimate the number of nights you'll stay in each park. Consider camping fees, hotel rates, or any other lodging options. Remember to book accommodations well in advance, especially during peak seasons. Yellowstone offers various lodging options: Camping ranges from $20 for basic tent sites to $99 for full hookup sites, excluding tax. Lodging inside the park varies widely, from $125 for basic cabins to over $700 for suites at iconic lodges like the Old Faithful Inn or Lake Yellowstone Lodge. Hotels outside the park offer similar rates. Generally, independent travelers average daily cost for accommodation in Yellowstone & Grand Teton National Parks is approximately $148 and $159 respectively for a double-occupancy room. Options range from rustic cabins to comfortable lodges, with prices varying based on location, amenities, and seasonality. You can expect to find accommodations in areas such as Colter Bay Village, Jenny Lake, and Signal Mountain.

4. FOOD: Plan your meals during your stay by considering various options such as dining in restaurants, cooking your meals if camping, or a mix of both. Take into account expenses for groceries, dining out, and any unique culinary experiences you wish to indulge in. Dining choices within the parks offer a range of prices, with grill lunches starting at approximately $10 and dinners costing between $15 and $40 per person. Opting to eat in nearby gateway towns can be more economical, with grocery shopping outside the park providing better prices and a wider selection, ideal for daytime picnics. On average, expect to spend around $46 per day on meals. While park dining options are available, they can be pricey relative to the food quality. Most restaurants serve American cuisine, though some offer international dishes on the park periphery. Various dining venues are available, including dining rooms, cafeterias, snack bars, and delis. It's advisable to stock up on supplies from general stores or trading posts, especially if you plan outdoor activities. Bringing your own food or picnicking amidst the parks' breathtaking scenery can help manage dining expenses while creating lasting culinary memories.

5. ENTERTAINMENT AND ACTIVITIES: Budget for any tours, guided activities, or entrance fees to specific attractions within the parks. Include costs for recreational activities like boat rentals, guided hikes, or ranger-led programs. Immersing yourself in the natural wonders of Grand Teton & Yellowstone National Parks comes with minimal costs, as entrance to the parks itself is the primary expense for sightseeing and outdoor activities. On average, travelers allocate around $43 for Grand Teton & $34 for Yellowstone per person per day for entertainment, covering admission fees to attractions, guided tours, and recreational pursuits such as hiking, canoeing, wildlife viewing and photography. Additional expenses may include optional activities like guided kayak tours or e-bike adventures.

6. GEAR AND EQUIPMENT: Factor in any additional gear you might need, such as camping equipment, hiking gear, or specialized clothing. Consider purchasing or renting gear if you don't already own it.

Depending on your existing gear, you may need to purchase specialized clothing, sun protection, rain gear, etc. Factor in costs for comfortable and practical items for outdoor activities.

6. VACATION PACKAGES: All-inclusive packages can simplify planning but come at a higher cost. Prices vary widely based on the duration of the trip, desired level of luxury, and included amenities. Day tours start at around $335 per person, while multi-day packages can range from $900 to $5,000 or more per person, excluding tax and tips.

7. ALCOHOL: Indulging in alcoholic beverages adds an average of $19 per day to the overall travel budget on both parks. While not a significant expense for everyone, enjoying a drink or two can enhance the overall experience, especially when unwinding after a day of exploration.

6. MISCELLANEOUS EXPENSES: Include any miscellaneous expenses like park souvenirs, park passes, or unexpected costs.

Once you've estimated these costs, add them up to get the total combined cost of visiting both Yellowstone and Grand Teton National Parks together. Keep in mind that actual costs may vary depending on factors such as travel preferences, accommodation choices, and individual spending habits.

The cost of visiting Yellowstone and Grand Teton National Parks can vary significantly depending on individual preferences, from frugal camping trips to extravagant vacation packages. Planning ahead and considering all expenses can help ensure a memorable and budget-conscious adventure in one of America's most iconic national parks.

HOW TO GET THERE

Yellowstone National Park and Grand Teton National Park are located in the western United States, primarily in Wyoming. Below are the main transportation options:

BY AIR: The closest major airports to Yellowstone are Jackson Hole Airport (JAC) near Grand Teton National Park and Bozeman Yellowstone International Airport (BZN) in Montana. From these airports, you can rent a car or use shuttle services to reach the parks.

TRAVELING FROM CANADA, EUROPE, NEW ZEALAND, AUSTRALIA, ASIA, AND AFRICA: *Flight:* Most likely, your journey will start with a flight to a major airport in the United States like New York (JFK), Chicago (ORD), or Los Angeles (LAX), SFO, or SEA (Seattle). From there, catch a connecting flight to Bozeman Yellowstone International Airport (BZN) or Jackson Hole Airport (JAC) for access to both parks. | *Driving:* If you prefer a scenic road trip, you could rent a car from one of these airports and drive to Yellowstone. It's a picturesque journey through the Rocky Mountains, and you can enter the park from various entrances depending on your route. | To Grand Teton: Follow the same steps as above for reaching Yellowstone, as Grand Teton National Park is located just south of Yellowstone. You can explore both parks together during your trip.

VISA REQUIREMENTS: Ensure you have the necessary visas for entry into the United States, which may vary based on your nationality and the purpose/duration of your visit. Check with the US embassy or consulate in your country for specific visa requirements here: *https://www.usembassy.gov*

BY CAR: Both parks are accessible by car. Major highways leading to the parks include US-89, US-191, and US-20. It's important to note that road closures may occur in winter, so check for updates and plan accordingly. Use *https://www.wyoroad.info* for updates.

PARK REGULATIONS AND PERMITS

When visiting Yellowstone and Grand Teton National Parks, it's essential to adhere to park regulations to ensure the safety of visitors, protect the natural environment, and preserve the parks for future generations. Here are some key regulations to keep in mind:

GENERAL REGULATIONS

1. Follow Park Rules: Obey all posted signs and regulations throughout the parks.

2. Stay on Designated Trails: Stick to designated trails and boardwalks to protect fragile ecosystems and minimize damage to vegetation.

3. Pack Out Trash: Practice Leave No Trace principles by carrying out all trash and disposing of it properly. This helps keep the parks clean and protects wildlife from ingesting harmful materials.

4. Wildlife Viewing: Keep a safe distance from wildlife and never approach or feed them. Maintain a distance of at least 100 yards from bears and wolves and 25 yards from all other wildlife.

5. Campfire Regulations: Follow park guidelines for campfires, including using established fire rings in designated campgrounds and adhering to any fire restrictions in place.

6. Camping Regulations: Camp only in designated campsites and obtain necessary permits for backcountry camping. Follow all guidelines for food storage to prevent wildlife encounters.

YELLOWSTONE-SPECIFIC REGULATIONS

1. Geothermal Areas: Stay on boardwalks and designated paths in geothermal areas. The ground may be thin and fragile, and hot springs and geysers can cause severe burns.

2. Boating Regulations: Follow boating regulations on Yellowstone Lake, including speed limits and restrictions on certain areas to protect wildlife and minimize disturbance.

3. Fishing Regulations: Obtain a fishing permit and follow regulations regarding catch limits, gear restrictions, and seasonal closures.

4. Road Rules: Adhere to speed limits and traffic rules on park roads, and be aware of wildlife crossings, especially during dawn and dusk when animals are most active.

GRAND TETON-SPECIFIC REGULATIONS

1. Climbing Regulations: Follow climbing regulations in Grand Teton National Park, including registering for climbs, obtaining necessary permits, and adhering to route closures for nesting raptors.

2. Backcountry Permits: Obtain permits for backcountry camping and adhere to regulations regarding campsite selection, food storage, and waste disposal.

3. River and Lake Activities: Follow regulations for boating, kayaking, and other water activities on the Snake River and Jackson Lake, including permits and safety requirements.

4. Wilderness Camping: If camping in the Teton Wilderness, follow specific regulations for bear-proof food storage and camping in designated zones.

IMPORTANT NOTES

- Always prioritize safety and respect for the natural environment when visiting these parks.
- Be mindful of weather conditions, especially in mountainous areas where weather can change rapidly.
- Educate yourself about park regulations before your visit to ensure a memorable and enjoyable experience while minimizing impact on the environment.

It's essential to familiarize yourself with the regulations and guidelines provided by the National Park Service to ensure a safe and responsible visit to the parks.

CHAPTER 2: THE GATEWAY TOWNS TO YELLOWSTONE AND GRAND TETON NATIONAL PARKS

Jackson Hole, WY
West Yellowstone, MT
Bozeman, MT
Cody, WY
Gardiner, MT
Big Sky, MT
East Yellowstone, WY
Cooke City, MT
Livingston, MT
Red Lodge, MT
Ennis, MT
Island Park, ID
Dubois, WY

JACKSON HOLE, WY

Jackson Hole, Wyoming is situated just south of Grand Teton National Park, Jackson serves as an ideal hub for exploring Yellowstone via its South Entrance. Not only does it provide convenient access to these iconic parks, but it's also renowned as a gateway community. If you are a winter enthusiasts, Jackson boasts one of the premier ski areas in the nation, Jackson Hole Mountain Resort. Meanwhile, during the warmer months, You can immerse yourself in the charming western ambiance of downtown Jackson. From rafting and hiking to fishing, outdoor adventures abound, with the Jackson Town Square serving as a bustling focal point. Don't miss the chance to snap a photo beneath the iconic antler arch, savor delectable cuisine at nearby eateries, or catch the lively summer shootout performances.

LOCATION

Jackson, Wyoming sits in the western region of the state, nestled south of Grand Teton National Park and slightly east of the

Wyoming-Idaho border. Positioned just over an hour's drive south of Yellowstone's South Entrance, it serves as a convenient gateway to both iconic parks. The closest airports are Jackson Hole Airport (JAC) and Idaho Falls (IDA), located approximately 1.5 hours to the west.

AMENITIES & SERVICES AVAILABLE IN JACKSON HOLE

In Jackson, despite its modest year-round population of just under 10,000 residents, you'll discover a charming blend of small-town warmth alongside a robust offering of urban conveniences. Primarily fueled by tourism, Jackson caters to visitors with an extensive selection of dining establishments, lodging options, and a diverse range of activities and attractions. From cozy eateries to upscale dining experiences, accommodations ranging from boutique hotels to rustic lodges, and a plethora of recreational pursuits, there's something for everyone. While you won't find a sprawling shopping mall, Jackson compensates with its unique boutiques and specialty shops, adding to the town's distinct character and appeal.

WHAT TO DO AND SEE IN JACKSON HOLE

In Jackson, there's an abundance of activities and sights to explore, ensuring a memorable experience for you: **1. Grand Teton National Park:** Just a stone's throw north of town, this majestic park beckons with its scenic trails and breathtaking vistas. Whether you opt for a leisurely hike through the canyons or prefer to admire the views from a tranquil float trip, there's no shortage of natural wonders to discover. | **2. Jackson Hole Mountain Resort:** Renowned as one of the premier ski destinations, this resort offers adrenaline-pumping adventures in the winter, including exhilarating tram rides and epic skiing opportunities. In the summer, the resort transforms into a playground for outdoor enthusiasts, offering mountain biking, hiking trails, and scenic tram rides to soak in the stunning panoramas. | **3. Town Square:** Serving as the bustling epicenter of Jackson Hole, the Town Square brims with a vibrant array of restaurants, shops, and entertainment options, making it a must-visit destination for tourists and locals alike. | **4. National Elk Refuge:**

During the winter months, witness the spectacle of a massive elk herd at the Elk Refuge, located just north of town. Embark on a magical sleigh ride through the refuge to get up close with these majestic creatures in their natural habitat. | **5. Fishing:** Anglers will delight in the abundance of prime fishing spots, including the Snake River, Hoback River, Flat Creek, and Gros Ventre River, renowned for their superb fly fishing opportunities. For a scenic adventure, consider floating the South Fork of the Snake River in Swan Valley. | **6. Rafting:** Experience the thrill of whitewater rafting in the Snake River Canyon or opt for a leisurely scenic float trip within Grand Teton National Park or just south of it, soaking in the picturesque landscapes along the way. | **7. Hiking and Biking:** Lace up your hiking boots and explore the picturesque trails of Grand Teton National Park, or hop on a mountain bike to tackle the exhilarating trails of Teton Pass and Cache Creek. | **8. Snowmobiling:** Embrace the winter wonderland by embarking on a thrilling snowmobiling adventure at Togwotee Pass or join a guided tour to explore the enchanting landscapes of Yellowstone's south entrance.

WEST YELLOWSTONE, MT

West Yellowstone is situated right at the West Entrance to Yellowstone National Park, it offers unparalleled convenience for exploring this natural wonder. As a quintessential tourist hub, the downtown area boasts a charming array of souvenir shops, eateries, and accommodations, ensuring a comfortable and enjoyable stay. Beyond its proximity to the park, West Yellowstone also features several unique attractions just a stone's throw away. Immerse yourself in the world of wildlife at the Grizzly and Wolf Discovery Center, catch a captivating IMAX documentary, or delve into the region's rich history at the Yellowstone Historic Center. With its blend of accessibility and engaging attractions, West Yellowstone promises an unforgettable experience for visitors of all ages.

LOCATION: West Yellowstone is situated just outside the West Entrance to Yellowstone National Park. It sits approximately 50 miles south of Big Sky, 90 miles south of Bozeman, and about 100 miles northeast of Idaho Falls. While West Yellowstone does have a seasonal airport, the closest major airport is located in Bozeman.

AMENITIES & SERVICES AVAILABLE: In West Yellowstone, you'll find everything tailored to the tourist experience. Choose from a diverse range of lodging options, including hotels, motels, lodges and cozy cabins, ensuring a comfortable stay for every traveler. While the culinary scene may not offer a wide array of cuisine types, numerous restaurants & delightful ice cream parlors cater to various tastes. Dive into the vibrant shopping scene with gear shops & souvenir stores lining the streets, offering an array of mementos & outdoor essentials. Additionally, there's a main grocery store to fulfill any provisioning needs during your visit.

WHAT TO DO & SEE IN
WEST YELLOWSTONE

While in West Yellowstone, there's a wealth of attractions and activities to explore, ensuring an enriching and memorable visit:

1. Grizzly and Wolf Discovery Center: Delve into the world of bears and wolves at this fascinating animal sanctuary. Witness these majestic creatures up close and even schedule your visit during feeding times. Open year-round for your enjoyment. | **2. IMAX Theater:** Immerse yourself in captivating cinematic experiences on an enormous screen. Choose from a selection of seasonal features or opt for the timeless Yellowstone movie, offering an awe-inspiring journey through the park's natural wonders. | **3. Yellowstone Historic Center:** Step back in time at the Yellowstone Historic Center, housed in the historic train depot. Explore a comprehensive display of local history and don't forget to grab a Historic Walking Tour Pamphlet for an immersive journey through the town's heritage. | **4. Hebgen Lake:** Just a short drive north of West Yellowstone, Hebgen Lake beckons with its scenic beauty and recreational opportunities, attracting boaters, anglers, and families seeking a picturesque spot for picnics or camping. | **5. Quake Lake:** Further along the road from Hebgen Lake lies Quake Lake, formed by a massive earthquake. Visit the visitor center to learn about its intriguing geological history or enjoy camping along its tranquil shores. | **6. Madison River:** Anglers rejoice in the exceptional trout fishing waters of the Madison River, stretching from Madison Junction in Yellowstone to Three Forks, Montana, offering endless opportunities for outdoor enthusiasts. | **7. Riverside Trails:** Embark on scenic hikes right from town, with trails accessible year-round. In winter, these trails transform into a winter wonderland, perfect for cross-country skiing adventures. | **8. Winter in Yellowstone:** Embrace the magic of winter in Yellowstone, where the hub of activity thrives in West Yellowstone. While road access into the park is limited during winter, embark on guided snowmobiling tours or snowcoach rides to marvel at the park's snowy landscapes and iconic attractions, including the legendary Old Faithful geyser.

BOZEMAN, MT

Bozeman is a vibrant college town that boasts a distinctive blend of character and charm that's hard to resist. Indulge in a diverse culinary scene, with an array of restaurants catering to every palate, alongside a variety of lodging options and traveler services ensuring a comfortable stay. Bozeman's cultural calendar brims with engaging community events, from live music and theater performances to bustling farmer's markets and monthly art walks through downtown. If you are an Outdoor enthusiasts, you will find yourself in paradise, with easy access to hiking trails in the Gallatin and Bridger Mountain Ranges, world-class fly fishing rivers, and exhilarating skiing opportunities at Bridger Bowl. If you seek summer adventures or winter thrills, Bozeman serves as an ideal basecamp for exploring the wonders of Yellowstone National Park and beyond.

LOCATION

Bozeman, Montana, is situated in the southwestern part of the state, nestled just north of Yellowstone National Park. You can access the park via two main entrances: the north entrance, approximately 80 miles southeast of Bozeman in Gardiner, Montana, or the west entrance, roughly 89 miles south of Bozeman in West Yellowstone,

Montana.

AMENITIES & SERVICES AVAILABLE IN BOZEMAN, MT

Bozeman offers a diverse array of services and amenities with accommodation options ranging from well-known hotel chains and motels to cozy bed and breakfasts and RV parks. Dining choices are abundant, featuring a wide selection of cuisines to satisfy any palate. During the summer months, you can enjoy browsing through the fresh produce at local farmer's markets. Downtown Bozeman boasts a charming collection of boutique shops and galleries. To Yellowstone National Park, the Gallatin Field Airport serves as a convenient gateway. With connections to major cities regionally and nationally, it provides easy access to the area. Rental car services are available at the airport, or you can opt for bus rides or guided tours to explore the park.

WHAT TO DO & SEE IN
BOZEMAN, MT

Discover Yellowstone National Park: Experience the wonders of Yellowstone through the north or west entrances, whether embarking on a day trip or indulging in a multi-day adventure after stocking up on supplies in Bozeman. | **Hit the Slopes at Bridger Bowl:** Enjoy the affordable skiing at Bridger Bowl, where you'll find excellent value for your skiing experience. | **Explore the Museum of the Rockies:** Delve into the extensive paleontology collection, the largest in the world, at the Museum of the Rockies, conveniently located in Bozeman.

| **Conquer the M Trail:** Challenge yourself with the popular M Trail hike, offering breathtaking views of Bozeman and its surrounding mountains from the iconic M overlook. | **Relax at Norris Hot Springs:** Unwind at Norris Hot Springs, southwest of Bozeman, especially delightful during the cooler seasons, with the added bonus of live music on weekend evenings. | **Cast a Line in the Gallatin River:** Experience world-class fly fishing in the Gallatin River, earning Bozeman its reputation as a haven for anglers. | **Adventure in Hyalite Canyon:** Explore the hiking, biking, and climbing opportunities in Hyalite Canyon, just a stone's throw from Bozeman. During winter, marvel at or participate in the thrilling ice climbing experiences available.

<u>CODY, WY</u>

Situated in the eastern region of Yellowstone National Park, Cody, Wyoming, emerges as a vibrant western destination renowned for its lively summer rodeo events. Why consider a visit to Cody, Wyoming? This historic town, paying homage to the legendary figure Buffalo Bill Cody, encapsulates the essence of America's pioneering spirit. Rich in history and brimming with charm, Cody beckons visitors with its plethora of outdoor activities. From fishing and hiking to camping amidst picturesque mountain ranges, adventure awaits. Scenic drives like Chief Joseph and Beartooth Pass offer captivating vistas deserving of a day's exploration. Plus, during the summer months, easy access to Yellowstone National Park via the east entrance adds another layer of allure to this captivating destination.

<u>LOCATION:</u> Cody resides in the northwest region of Wyoming, positioned directly east of the east entrance of Yellowstone National Park. Traveling from Cody to the park's east entrance typically takes approximately an hour.

<u>AMENITIES & SERVICES AVAILABLE:</u> In Cody, you'll find a diverse array of services & amenities catering to different preferences. Choose from a wide selection of lodging options ranging from chain hotels & motels to charming bed & breakfasts & nearby guest ranches. Dining options abound, with menus featuring delicious offerings such as ribs, steaks, and burgers, along with a variety of other cuisines to suit every palate. Shopping in Cody is a delightful experience, offering everything from cowboy boots & hats to unique gifts & souvenirs, ensuring you'll find the perfect memento.

WHAT TO SEE & DO IN CODY

In Cody, there's no shortage of exciting activities and attractions to explore: *1. Cody Nite Rodeo:* Experience the thrill of nightly rodeos held at Stampede Park throughout June, July, and August, offering an authentic taste of western culture. | *2. Yellowstone National Park:* Just a little over an hour's drive west from Cody lies the east entrance to Yellowstone National Park, accessible during the summer season only, where you can marvel at breathtaking natural wonders and abundant wildlife. | *3. Buffalo Bill Historical Center:* Immerse yourself in the captivating narratives of the western frontier at this renowned museum, delving into the rich history of Wyoming and the legendary figure Buffalo Bill Cody. | *4. Buffalo Bill State Park:* Spend a leisurely day amidst the picturesque landscapes of Buffalo Bill Reservoir and state park grounds, offering a serene environment for outdoor recreation and relaxation. | *5. Clark's Fork of the Yellowstone River:* Embark on a fishing adventure in the remote and scenic Clark's Fork area, accessible via the Chief Joseph Scenic Byway, where pristine waters teem with trout amidst majestic mountain vistas. | *6. Chief Joseph Scenic Byway:* Hit the road north from Cody on WY 120 to embark on the scenic Chief Joseph Byway, offering stunning vistas and opportunities for exploration. You can opt for a leisurely out-and-back drive or combine it with the iconic Beartooth Pass route, returning through Red Lodge during the summer months for an extended journey filled with breathtaking scenery.

GARDINER, MT

Gardiner, Montana, situated just outside the North Entrance of Yellowstone National Park, provides a convenient hub for visiting the park offering a range of lodging options, dining establishments, and a variety of activities to enhance the Yellowstone experience. Gardiner stands out as a must-visit destination for its unique status as Yellowstone's sole year-round entrance for vehicles, making it an ideal winter getaway for park enthusiasts. Nestled at the southern boundary of Paradise Valley and bordered by the majestic Yellowstone River, Gardiner boasts a plethora of attractions and activities, ensuring an unforgettable experience year-round.

LOCATION: Gardiner is situated adjacent to Yellowstone's North Entrance, serving as the closest neighbor to Mammoth Hot Springs within the park. Positioned approximately an hour south of Livingston, Montana, Gardiner offers convenient access to the wonders of Yellowstone National Park.

AMENITIES & SERVICES AVAILABLE: In Gardiner, you can enjoy a range of services and amenities to enhance your stay, including several motels and a couple of campgrounds for accommodation options. Additionally, the town features a small airport, a grocery store for convenient shopping, as well as souvenir shops and art galleries for unique keepsakes and local artwork. Dining options in Gardiner encompass a modest variety of restaurants, ensuring satisfying meals during your visit.

WHAT TO SEE & DO IN GARDINER, MT

In Gardiner, there's no shortage of captivating sights and activities to enjoy: **1. Scenic Drive through Paradise Valley:** Embark on a picturesque journey north of Gardiner, traversing through the breathtaking landscapes of Paradise Valley, renowned for its stunning vistas and serene beauty. | **2. Chico Hot Springs:** Just a short drive north of Gardiner, immerse yourself in relaxation at Chico Hot Springs in the heart of Paradise Valley. Indulge in a rejuvenating soak in the natural hot springs and consider extending your stay at the onsite hotel, complete with a fantastic restaurant offering delectable dining options. | **3. Yellowstone River:** Flowing through Gardiner, the Yellowstone River presents excellent opportunities for fly fishing and rafting adventures, allowing visitors to experience the thrill of outdoor exploration amidst pristine natural surroundings. | **4. Hiking:** With the Absaroka Mountain Range and Yellowstone National Park as its backdrop, Gardiner boasts an array of hiking trails suitable for all skill levels, offering opportunities to immerse yourself in the beauty of the surrounding wilderness. | **5. Mammoth Hot Springs Area:** Venture into Yellowstone National Park and explore the wonders of the Mammoth Hot Springs area, where you'll encounter fascinating geological formations, including terraces. Additionally, don't miss the chance to visit Fort Yellowstone, relax in the Boiling River soaking area, and explore a variety of hiking and cross-country skiing trails, all within easy reach from Gardiner.

BIG SKY, MT

Big Sky, Montana, nestled in the Madison Range near Yellowstone National Park, offers upscale accommodations and activities for all budgets year-round. From hiking, biking, rafting, and fishing to golfing and family-friendly entertainment, it caters to diverse interests. In winter, it becomes a haven for winter sports enthusiasts, with skiing and luxurious amenities. Big Sky Resort, with the largest skiing terrain in America, combines the areas of Big Sky and Moonlight Basin. Beyond skiing, it offers fly fishing, mountain biking, golf, and easy access to Yellowstone Park, attracting summer visitors too.

LOCATION: Big Sky Montana is situated in the scenic Gallatin River Canyon, approximately equidistant from West Yellowstone to the south and Bozeman to the north. The turnoff for Big Sky lies at the base of the canyon alongside the Gallatin River. From there, the resort, Town Center, and Meadow Village are easily accessible via a short drive up the hill into the majestic Madison Mountain Range.

AMENITIES & SERVICES AVAILABLE: Accommodation choices abound, ranging from luxurious hotels & resorts conveniently located near the ski resort's base area to numerous vacation rentals & condos. The term "motel" isn't commonly used in Big Sky, reflecting its upscale atmosphere. For RVs & tent campers, there are several

Forest Service campgrounds lining the Gallatin River, just a short drive from the heart of Big Sky. Within Big Sky, you'll find a couple of small yet upscale grocery stores situated in Town Center & Meadow Village, catering to residents and visitors. The dining scene boasts numerous delightful restaurants offering diverse culinary experiences. If you seek the big-city amenities & services, Bozeman, Montana, located north of Big Sky, provides a broader range of options.

WHAT TO SEE & DO IN BIG SKY, MT

1. Yellowstone National Park: Just over an hour's drive north from the West Entrance, Big Sky provides easy access to several trailheads along the northwest corner of Yellowstone, ideal for backpacking or hiking away from the crowds. | **2. Skiing/Snowboarding:** Winter is prime time in Big Sky, with the resort now incorporating Moonlight Basin, offering extensive terrain for skiing and snowboarding enthusiasts. | **3. Fly Fishing:** Situated uphill from the Gallatin River, Big Sky is a haven for anglers seeking pristine fishing spots. | **4. Kid-Friendly Activities:** Beyond skiing and gentle hiking trails, Big Sky offers an array of family-friendly activities such as zip-lining, frisbee golf, a climbing wall, bungee trampoline, and more. | **5. Mountain Biking:** Big Sky boasts top-notch lift-accessible trails, perfect for downhill and all-mountain biking adventures. | **6. Hiking:** Embark on the Ousel Falls trail for an easy hike leading to a stunning waterfall, or opt for a longer trek into Beehive Basin, nestled below the Spanish Peaks. | **7. Cross-Country Skiing:** Lone Mountain Ranch is a Nordic skiing and snowshoeing paradise in the winter, offering cabin accommodations or day passes for enthusiasts. | **8. Annual Events:** During the summer, enjoy free Music in the Mountains & weekly Farmer's Markets, which are beloved by locals & visitors alike.

OTHER NEARBY TOWNS

1. EAST YELLOWSTONE, WY

East Yellowstone, situated near the East Entrance of Yellowstone National Park, offers a serene retreat with access to some of the best lodges and guest ranches in the area. Despite being more of an area than a town, it provides a picturesque setting along the North Fork of the Shoshone River, making it an ideal destination for outdoor enthusiasts. In East Yellowstone, you can enjoy a range of activities, including fishing along the North Fork of the Shoshone River, known for its superb fly fishing opportunities, or at Buffalo Bill Reservoir, ideal for spin rods. Horseback riding in the Shoshone National Forest, guided by lodges and guest ranches, offers a unique way to explore the surrounding wilderness. If you are an Hiking enthusiast, you can explore endless trails within Yellowstone Park or along the drainages lining the North Fork Hwy. For entertainment, you can attend the Cody Nite Rodeo in nearby Cody during the summer months, experiencing the thrill of this western tradition. While services and amenities are limited in East Yellowstone, with no gas stations, grocery stores, or ATMs available in the area, you can find these conveniences in Cody, Wyoming, or within Yellowstone National Park. However, East Yellowstone offers a tranquil escape amidst nature, with its scenic beauty and abundant outdoor recreational opportunities attracting travelers seeking a peaceful retreat. Additionally, nearby attractions like Buffalo Bill State Park, with its historical center, reservoir, and park facilities, provide further opportunities for exploration and enjoyment.

2. COOKE CITY, MT

Cooke City, Montana, located just outside the northeast entrance of Yellowstone National Park, offers a serene retreat with fewer crowds and personalized hospitality. As the quietest gateway town to the park, it provides charm, some services, and easy access to outdoor recreation. In summer, you can reach Cooke City from both the west (Yellowstone) and east (Beartooth Pass), with the latter offering breathtaking views along the Beartooth Highway. During winter, Cooke City becomes a peaceful destination with limited access to the park. Despite its small size, Cooke City offers essential services such as a visitor center, ATM, gas stations, a small grocery store, snowmobile rentals, and guide services. Dining options include several restaurants and popular saloons, while lodging options range from motels to bed and breakfasts. You can explore Yellowstone National Park easily from Cooke City, especially for wildlife viewing in Lamar Valley and hiking trails. In winter, snowmobiling and cross-country skiing are popular activities, while in the summer you can enjoy the scenic Beartooth Pass Scenic Byway and fly fishing in nearby rivers. Additionally, camping options are available in national forest service campgrounds along the highway east of Cooke City, offering a rustic outdoor experience.

3. LIVINGSTON, MT

Livingston, Montana, nestled among the Crazys, Absarokas, and Bridgers mountain ranges and bordered by the Yellowstone River, offers a charming small-town experience with access to big-city amenities. Serving as a primary gateway to Yellowstone's North Entrance, it sits in its picturesque valley, just 55 miles north of the park. Its downtown area boasts art galleries, unique shops, and a variety of dining options.

Despite its small size, Livingston offers a range of amenities and services comparable to a big city. Accommodation options include hotels and motels, while restaurants and shops are predominantly located downtown. For recreation, the Yellowstone River is renowned for fly fishing between Gardiner and Livingston. Nearby, Chico Hot Springs in Paradise Valley offers a historic hotel with hot springs pools, dining, and live music. You can also explore the area's history at the Livingston Depot Center, which features exhibits on the Northern Pacific Railroad. If you are an outdoor enthusiast, you will find endless hiking opportunities in the surrounding mountain ranges, with trails like Pine Creek Falls and Passage Falls offering scenic routes. For entertainment, the Center for the Arts and the Blue Slipper Theatre provide cultural experiences through theatrical performances. Whether it's outdoor adventures, cultural attractions, or simply soaking in the scenic beauty, Livingston offers something for every traveler.

4. RED LODGE, MT

Red Lodge, Montana, nestled at the base of the Beartooth Mountains, offers a unique and picturesque setting for outdoor enthusiasts. Serving as a gateway to Yellowstone via the seasonal Beartooth Highway, the town is renowned for its stunning scenic drive, considered one of the most beautiful in the country. While small, Red Lodge provides a charming atmosphere with a selection of accommodations, dining options, and shops along Broadway Avenue. *Accommodation options* in Red Lodge include motels, hotels, lodges, and bed and breakfasts, catering to various preferences and budgets. Dining options range from local eateries to specialty food shops, ensuring a diverse culinary experience. Basic amenities such as gas stations, a grocery store, post office, and ATMs are also available.

You can embark on scenic drives along the *Beartooth Highway*, taking in breathtaking views of the surrounding mountains and valleys. *Red Lodge Mountain Resort* offers skiing and snowboarding opportunities during the winter months, attracting outdoor enthusiasts seeking snowy adventures. For a taste of nostalgia, *the Candy Emporium* in downtown Red Lodge is a popular stop for satisfying sweet cravings. If you are with family, you can enjoy a visit to the *Beartooth Nature Center*, home to animals unable to return to the wild, providing educational and entertaining experiences. *Wild Bill Lake* offers a tranquil setting for picnics and fishing, while hiking trails like the **West Fork Trail** provide opportunities for exploration and outdoor recreation. **During the summer months**, you can partake in the **Bear Creek Pig Races** at the Bear Creek Saloon, providing fun and entertainment for all ages. Red Lodge offers a premier destination for memorable experiences amidst the beauty of the Beartooth Mountains whether it's scenic drives, outdoor activities, or unique attractions,

5. ENNIS, MT

Ennis, Montana, nestled in the heart of the Madison River Valley, offers a vibrant small-town experience with a plethora of outdoor recreational opportunities. While its population may be small, Ennis boasts a lively downtown, an artistic community, and a calendar filled with events, making it feel bustling and dynamic. Situated along one of the scenic drives linking Bozeman to Yellowstone National Park, Ennis provides easy access to the surrounding natural beauty. You can reach Ennis from Bozeman via U.S. 287, passing through Four Corners and Norris before arriving in Ennis, roughly an hour's drive. From Ennis, you can continue on to Yellowstone via different routes, each offering scenic vistas and unique landscapes.

Ennis offers a range of services and amenities to accommodate visitors, including lodging options, dining establishments, small shops, mini-marts, gas stations, ATMs, and a post office, ensuring a comfortable stay for travelers. If you are an Outdoor enthusiast, you will find plenty to do and see in Ennis and its surroundings. **Fly fishing** is a popular activity on the upper Madison River, while Ennis Lake, **Hebgen Lake**, and **Henry's Lake** provide opportunities for both fly and spin rod fishing. **Hiking trails** abound in the surrounding mountains, offering breathtaking views and diverse terrain. **Rafting** trips through Beartrap Canyon, just north of Ennis Lake, provide thrilling adventures on the water. **Nearby attractions** include the historic ghost town of **Virginia City**, just 11 miles west of Ennis, and the *Lewis and Clark Caverns*, a short drive north, offering fascinating underground exploration. For relaxation, *Norris Hot Springs* offers rejuvenating hot springs baths and live music on weekend nights, providing a perfect way to unwind after a day of adventure. Ennis offers something for every traveler to enjoy whether it's outdoor activities, cultural exploration, or simply soaking in the natural beauty,

6. ISLAND PARK, ID

Island Park, nestled in western Idaho and surrounded by natural beauty, offers an ideal retreat for both summer and winter getaways. With numerous vacation rentals and condos, it caters to self-sufficient travelers seeking tranquility and outdoor adventure. The area boasts a plethora of unique attractions and recreational opportunities, making it a sought-after destination for outdoor enthusiasts.

Located south of West Yellowstone, Montana, and north of Ashton, Idaho, Island Park provides easy access to nearby attractions such as Mesa Falls, Big Springs, Harriman State Park, and Henry's Lake. Fishing, hiking, and snowmobiling are popular activities in the area, with abundant opportunities for outdoor exploration and adventure. Despite its rural setting, Island Park offers a range of services and amenities to ensure a comfortable stay for visitors. While hotels and motels are limited, lodging options like condos, vacation rentals, and lodges are plentiful. Gas stations, gear rentals, and ATMs are available, although restaurants and grocery stores are relatively few, so it's advisable to stock up on supplies before arrival. *Island Park's 35-mile Main Street* means services are spread out, emphasizing the need for careful planning and preparation. However, the abundance of attractions and activities make the journey worthwhile. From *Harriman State Park to Mesa Falls Scenic Byway*, from *Island Park Reservoir to Henry's Lake State Park*, you can immerse yourself in nature and enjoy a variety of outdoor experiences. If you are a

Fishing enthusiast, you will find the Henry's Fork a prime destination, while camping opportunities abound in National Forest Service campgrounds scattered throughout the area. *In winter*, Island Park transforms into a snowmobiling mecca, rivaling West Yellowstone in popularity. Rentals and tours are available if you seek snowy adventures. Island Park offers endless opportunities for outdoor recreation and exploration amidst stunning natural surroundings whether it's hiking, fishing, camping, or snowmobiling,

7. DUBOIS, WY

Dubois, Wyoming, hailed as an authentic cowboy town, offers you a taste of the Old West coupled with abundant outdoor recreation opportunities. Nestled along the Wind River and surrounded by the Absaroka and Wind River Mountains, Dubois provides a picturesque escape from the bustle of city life, conveniently located just east of Togwotee Pass. While Dubois may not be the easiest place to reach, its rustic charm and tranquil surroundings make it a worthwhile destination. The town boasts numerous guest ranches, hotels, motels, bed and breakfasts, and RV parks, providing a range of lodging options. Dining options include coffee shops and sit-down restaurants serving comfort food, while essential services like grocery stores, banks, and post offices ensure convenience for travelers.

You can immerse yourself in the local culture by attending the Friday Night Rodeo or participating in square dancing at the Rustic Pine Tavern on summer Tuesday nights. Outdoor enthusiasts will find endless opportunities for hiking in the nearby Wind River Range, with trails easily accessible from town. *The National Bighorn Sheep Interpretive Center* offers insight into the region's wildlife, while the *Dubois Museum* showcases the area's unique history and heritage. If you are a fishing enthusiast, you can explore the upper reaches of the *Wind River*, renowned for its abundant fish populations. Dubois offers something for every traveler seeking an authentic Western experience amidst stunning landscapes and rich history, whether it's experiencing the local culture, exploring the great outdoors, or simply soaking in the natural beauty.

Grand Prismatic Spring, Yellowstone National Park (A Unesco World Heritage Site), Wyoming - Photo By Mike Goadfollow

CHAPTER 3: WHAT TO DO & SEE IN YELLOWSTONE

1. Top Must-See Attractions
2. The Lakes of Yellowstone
3. The Valleys of Yellowstone
4. Wildlife Watching
5. Outdoor Activities
6. Historic Sites and Museums
7. Other Natural Attractions To See in Yellowstone

TOP 10 ATTRACTIONS

Most Visitors to Yellowstone National Park often wonder, "What are the must-see sights in Yellowstone?" Given the park's vastness and diversity, with each visitor having unique interests and abilities, there's no simple answer. However, we've created a general list of Yellowstone's top attractions to help you start planning your visit.

This list serves as a helpful guide to get you started. **CLICK HERE** to access a map of the top 10 attractions in Yellowstone or enter this URL in your browser: *https://tinyurl.com/ynp-top10-map*

1. GRAND PRISMATIC SPRING

Grand Prismatic Spring Overlook - Image Authored
By Bernd Thaller from Graz, Austria

This breathtaking hot spring is renowned for its vibrant colors, which range from deep blue in the center to vibrant oranges and reds along the edges. The colors are caused by pigmented bacteria and thermophiles that thrive in the varying temperatures of the spring. Grand Prismatic is one of the largest hot springs in the world and the largest hot spring in the US. It is best viewed from the boardwalk that surrounds it, providing you with a stunning aerial perspective.

2. YELLOWSTONE LAKE

Yellowstone Lake at West Thumb, Yellowstone National Park,
Wyoming, USA - Photo by Wikimedia User Acroterion

The Yellowstone Lake spans an impressive 352.2 km², stands as the park's largest body of water. Its striking sapphire-blue waters reflect the surrounding mountains & forests, offering you breathtaking views. Yellowstone Lake is the largest high-elevation lake in North America and a focal point of the park. Its serene beauty offers opportunities for boating, kayaking, and fishing. The lake is known for its native Yellowstone cutthroat trout, making it a popular destination for anglers. Fishing is permitted in the park, but visitors must obtain a fishing permit and follow regulations.

3. GRAND CANYON OF THE YELLOWSTONE

Grand Canyon of the Yellowstone River (Yellowstone, Wyoming, USA - Photo by James St. John

The Grand Canyon of the Yellowstone stretches about 20 miles from the Upper Falls to the Tower Fall area. It has depths ranging from 800 to 1,200 feet & widths between 1,500 and 4,000 feet. Geologically young, it is estimated to be 10,000 to 14,000 years old, though few studies have been conducted, and their accuracy is questionable. The canyon was formed primarily through erosion, not glaciation. The Grand Canyon of the Yellowstone is one of the most breathtaking natural wonders within Yellowstone National Park, renowned for its stunning beauty & geological significance. Carved by the erosive forces of the Yellowstone River over thousands of years, the canyon stretches approximately 24 miles long & reaches depths of up to 1,200 feet, revealing colorful cliffs, dramatic waterfalls & unique rock formations. | **Activities To Do in the Canyon Village Area:** Discover natural highlights. | Explore geological features. | Visit historic sites. | Learn about the super-volcano at the canyon visitor center. | Participate in ranger-guided programs. | Hike through the canyon area.

KEY FEATURES AND HIGHLIGHTS OF THE GRAND CANYON

OF THE YELLOWSTONE:

1. LOWER FALLS: Plunging dramatically into the canyon, the Lower Falls is one of the most iconic waterfalls in the park. With a height of 308 feet, it is nearly twice as high as Niagara Falls. The falls can be viewed from several vantage points, including Artist Point and Red Rock Point, offering visitors awe-inspiring vistas of the cascading water against the backdrop of the canyon's sheer walls.

Yellowstone's Lower Falls - Photo Created By Bernard Spragg

The Upper Falls of the Yellowstone River in Yellowstone NP Authord BY Supercarwaar (https://commons.wikimedia.org/wiki/User:Tristan_Surtel)

2. UPPER FALLS: Located upstream from the Lower Falls, the Upper Falls is another impressive waterfall along the Yellowstone River. Though not as high as the Lower Falls, it is equally majestic, with a height of approximately 109 feet. You can admire the Upper Falls from overlooks along the North Rim Drive, providing panoramic views of the rushing water and surrounding canyon landscape.

3. BRINK OF THE LOWER FALLS TRAIL: If you seek a closer view of the Lower Falls, the Brink of the Lower Falls Trail offers a thrilling experience. This short but steep trail descends to a viewpoint near the top of the waterfall, where visitors can feel the spray of the mist and marvel at the sheer power of the rushing water as it plunges into the canyon below.

4. INSPIRATION POINT: Situated along the South Rim Drive, Inspiration Point lives up to its name, offering breathtaking panoramic views of the canyon & the Lower Falls. From this vantage point, you can appreciate the grandeur of the canyon's colorful cliffs, the meandering Yellowstone River, and the distant mountains beyond.

New pavement and railings at Brink of the Lower Falls Trail, Photo Created BY NPS Jacob W. Frank

Accessible viewing platform at Inspiration Point - Photo Created BY NPS/Neal Herbert

5. ARTIST POINT: Renowned for its spectacular vistas, Artist Point is arguably the most famous viewpoint in the Grand Canyon of the Yellowstone. Named for the many artists who have been inspired by its beauty, this overlook provides a picture-perfect view of the Lower Falls framed by the towering canyon walls, making it a favorite spot for photographers and visitors alike.

The Grand Canyon of the Yellowstone is not only a geological wonder but also a testament to the power of nature's forces and the enduring beauty of the American wilderness. Whether admired from its scenic overlooks or explored up close on its trails, the canyon never fails to leave a lasting impression on all who visit.

4. OLD FAITHFUL GEYSER & UPPER GEYSER BASIN

Old Faithful, Yellowstone - Photo by Mike GoadFollow

Yellowstone National Park boasts nearly 60% of the world's geysers, with the Upper Geyser Basin housing the highest concentration, including the renowned Old Faithful. Despite its name, Old Faithful's eruptions aren't perfectly predictable. Other notable geysers in this basin include Castle, Grand, Daisy, and Riverside. For a live view, check out the webcam. Old Faithful is Perhaps the most famous of Yellowstone's geothermal features, Old Faithful has been captivating visitors for generations. It earned its name due to its predictable eruptions, which occur roughly every 90 minutes. Crowds gather to witness this natural spectacle as Old Faithful shoots scalding water and steam high into the air, sometimes reaching heights of over a hundred feet. | **Activities To Do in the Old Faithful Area:** Observe natural attractions such as Old Faithful, Midway Geyser Basin, or the Firehole River. | Explore geological sites showcasing evidence of 600,000-year-old lava flows and the ice coverage from 13,000 years ago. | Visit historic landmarks like the Old Faithful Lodge. | Stop by the New Old Faithful Visitor Center. | Participate in ranger-led programs. | Enjoy day hikes.

5. HAYDEN VALLEY

Hayden Valley in Central Yellowstone is famous for its large bison population. Located north of the Lake area and Mud Volcano thermal area, it is an ideal habitat for bison, which are often seen grazing by the Yellowstone River. The valley is also a good spot to see other wildlife, including coyotes, waterfowl, grizzly bears, and wolves. Wildlife enthusiasts can use the various pullouts and overlooks along the park road or hike the 21-mile Mary Mountain Trail from Hayden Valley to Madison. The best times for wildlife viewing are during dawn and dusk, with early morning being particularly favorable. The valley is most accessible from spring through fall, while Lamar Valley is open to vehicles year-round.

6. MAMMOTH HOT SPRINGS

Situated in the northern part of the park, Mammoth Hot Springs is known for its striking terraces of travertine rock. Hot water from deep beneath the earth's surface flows through fractures in the limestone, depositing minerals and creating intricate formations. The terraces resemble cascading waterfalls frozen in stone, and you can walk along boardwalks to admire their beauty up close.

7. NORRIS GEYSER BASIN

As one of the hottest and most dynamic thermal areas in Yellowstone, Norris Geyser Basin offers a diverse array of hydrothermal features. You can explore steam vents, hot springs, and geysers, including Steamboat Geyser, the world's tallest active geyser. The landscape here is ever-changing, with new features appearing and old ones shifting over time.

Mammoth Hot Springs - Photo created By Frank J Haynes

8. LAMAR VALLEY

Situated in the park's northeastern corner, Lamar Valley, along the Lamar River, earns its moniker as America's Serengeti due to its abundant and easily observable populations of large animals. The area hosts renowned inhabitants such as the Junction Butte and Lamar Canyon wolf packs, attracting enthusiasts armed with spotting scopes hoping to witness these majestic canines in their element. Alongside wolves, the Lamar Valley is home to expansive herds of bison, pronghorn, badgers, grizzly bears, bald eagles, osprey, deer, and coyotes. Numerous pullouts line the road, facilitating wildlife observation, with visitors encouraged to utilize the nearest one upon spotting any active wildlife.

Norris Geyser Basin boardwalks and people - Photo Creator: Jacob W. Frank

9. TOWER FALL

Tower Fall is the most popular waterfall in Yellowstone after the Lower Falls of the Grand Canyon. It is located near the General Store, and a short walk leads to an overlook. For a closer view, you can take a short but steep hike down to the base of the waterfall. Tower Fall is also a popular destination in winter, accessible by cross-country skis or snowshoes along the road from Roosevelt Junction to Tower Fall. The frozen waterfall, encased in an ice dome, is a stunning sight during the colder months. Situated 17 miles north of Canyon and two miles south of Roosevelt, Tower Fall stands 132 feet tall in a canyon near the Tower Falls General Store. A steep, half-mile switchback trail leads to the bottom of the waterfall, and the same trail must be taken back up. Winter visitors should bring appropriate footwear for the icy conditions. The name "Tower" comes from the towering volcanic formations at the top of the falls.

Bison rut in Lamar Valley By NPS / Neal Herbert

10. LOWER GEYSER BASIN

The Lower Geyser Basin, covering about 11 square miles, is the largest geyser basin in Yellowstone National Park. This area features a variety of thermal attractions, including regularly erupting geysers, hot springs, and a unique mud pool that captivates visitors. In contrast, the Upper Geyser Basin spans only about one square mile. The thermal features in the Lower Geyser Basin are grouped in widely spaced clusters, with the Fountain Paint Pot area being the most accessible and interesting.

Yellowstone Tower Falls By Zechariah Judy

NOTABLE FEATURES IN THE LOWER GEYSER BASIN INCLUDE:

FOUNTAIN PAINT POT TRAIL: A short walk along this trail provides excellent examples of the thermal features in Yellowstone, including hot pools, fumaroles, erupting geysers, and easily accessible mud pots. The area is highly active, and there is almost always at least one geyser erupting. The trail takes about 30 minutes to complete, but parking can be challenging due to the small lot. These mud pots vary in consistency depending on recent rainfall, ranging from soupy to thick. They expanded significantly after the 1959 Hebgen Lake earthquake, leading to trail and parking lot relocations. | **GREAT FOUNTAIN GEYSER:** This is the only predicted geyser in the Lower Geyser Basin and the only one in Yellowstone that you can drive to. Predictions for its eruptions are available at the Old Faithful Visitor Center. The geyser erupts in bursts, reaching heights between 75 and 220 feet, and can last over an hour. | **CELESTINE POOL:** Known for its near-boiling water, this hot spring has claimed human lives, highlighting the dangers of Yellowstone's thermal features. | **CLEPSYDRA GEYSER:** Often erupting to 45 feet, this geyser was named for a mythical water clock due to its regular eruptions in the park's early history. It has been in a near-constant state of eruption since the 1959 Hebgen Lake Earthquake. | **FOUNTAIN GEYSER:** This beautiful geyser erupts every 4 to 15 hours, with energetic bursts reaching over 75 feet. It is usually the main performer in the area since the nearby Morning Geyser is typically dormant. | **FUMAROLES:** Located at higher elevations, these steam vents are found in the driest areas, while the wetter features, like hot pools and geysers, are at lower levels. | **JET GEYSER:** Erupting every 7 to 30 minutes to 20 feet, Jet Geyser's activity increases during eruptions of the nearby Fountain Geyser. | **LEATHER POOL:** Named for the thick brown bacterial mat in its lukewarm waters. | **MORNING GEYSER:** A rarely active geyser, It can reach heights of 200 feet when it does erupt. Its last active period was in 1994. | **RED SPOUTER:** This fumarole sometimes appears as a small geyser when water accumulates near its vent. | **SILEX SPRING:** A beautiful blue hot spring where steam jets into the pool from the vent at the bottom, collapsing quickly as it meets the cooler water. | **SIZZLER:** A small, recently formed geyser that has evolved from cracks in the sinter to a gaping hole, demonstrating the dynamic nature of geyser basins. | **SPASM GEYSER:** A small geyser located next to the boardwalk.

The Lower Geyser Basin offers a diverse array of thermal features and is a fascinating area to explore, showcasing the dynamic and ever-changing landscape of Yellowstone.

GEOTHERMAL MARVELS

Yellowstone National Park is famous for its geothermal features, which are a result of the park's location on top of a volcanic hotspot. These geothermal marvels include geysers, hot springs, mud pots, and fumaroles. The most renowned feature is Old Faithful, a predictable geyser that erupts approximately every 90 minutes, shooting hot water and steam high into the air. Other notable geysers in the park include the Grand Geyser, Castle Geyser, and Beehive Geyser. Exploring the colorful and unique hot springs, such as the Grand Prismatic Spring and the Morning Glory Pool, is also a must-do activity in Yellowstone.

TYPES OF HYDROTHERMAL FEATURES IN YELLOWSTONE: *Hot Springs:* Pools of hydrothermally heated water. | *Geysers:* Hot springs that periodically erupt due to constrictions in their plumbing. | *Mudpots:* Acidic hot springs that dissolve surrounding rock and lack water. | *Travertine Terraces:* Hot springs that dissolve calcium carbonate from limestone, forming terraces. | *Fumaroles:* Steam vents that release hot steam due to a lack of water.

NOTEWORTHY GEOTHERMAL FEATURES

MOST IMPRESSIVE: UPPER TERRACES: The Upper Terraces at Mammoth Hot Springs are known for their size and continuous growth, causing boardwalks to be frequently moved. The bright white and yellow terraces can be viewed from the 1.7 miles of boardwalks or by driving/cross-country skiing the Terrace Loop.

LOUDEST FROM THE INN: BEEHIVE GEYSER: Located in the Upper Geyser Basin, Beehive Geyser erupts about twice a day, reaching up to 200 feet and lasting 4-5 minutes. It is loud enough to be heard from inside the Old Faithful Inn.

MOST FUN TO WATCH - MUD POTS: The mud pots bubble, gurgle, and splatter, emitting a rotten egg smell due to hydrogen sulfide gas. They provide a calming and mesmerizing experience for visitors.

OLDEST - CASTLE GEYSER: With a 12-foot high cone, Castle Geyser has been building up for 5,000 to 15,000 years. It erupts every 9 to 11 hours, shooting water up to 90 feet.

MOST INTRIGUING - ANEMONE GEYSER: Anemone Geyser, resembling a draining bathtub, erupts every few minutes. It's a favorite for kids because they can get close and watch its cycle.

TALLEST - STEAMBOAT GEYSER: The tallest geyser in the world, Steamboat Geyser, can shoot water between 300 and 400 feet. It is highly unpredictable, with intervals between eruptions ranging from weeks to decades.

PRETTIEST - GRAND PRISMATIC & MORNING GLORY: **Grand Prismatic Spring:** Known for its deep blue center and orange edges, it is the largest hot spring in Yellowstone and the third largest in the world. A 0.6-mile hike to an overlook offers a stunning view. | **Morning Glory Pool:** Once affected by litter that cooled its waters and changed its colors, recent cleanup efforts have restored some of its vibrant hues.

These geothermal features demonstrate the incredible natural diversity and dynamic landscapes that make Yellowstone a must-visit destination.

MUD VOLCANO AREA

As its name suggests, this area of the park is characterized by bubbling mud pots, fumaroles, and hot springs. The landscape is otherworldly, with pools of boiling mud and steam vents hissing and gurgling amidst the barren terrain. One of the notable features here is the Dragon's Mouth Spring, where water surges in and out of a cave, creating the illusion of a dragon breathing steam.

Mud Volcano - Author By InSapphoWeTrust from Los Angeles, California, USA

These geothermal marvels are not only stunning to behold but also serve as reminders of the dynamic forces at work beneath the earth's surface. Visitors to Yellowstone National Park are treated to a unique glimpse into the power and beauty of the natural world, where geothermal activity shapes the landscape in awe-inspiring ways.

YELLOWSTONE LAKES

SHOSHONE LAKE, covering 32.58 km², is the park's second-largest lake, nestled amidst dense forests and rugged peaks. Accessible primarily by hiking or boating, it provides a tranquil escape from the crowds, rewarding adventurers with its serene atmosphere and untouched wilderness.

LEWIS LAKE is renowned for its pristine waters and thriving trout populations, attracting anglers from far and wide. Surrounded by majestic lodgepole pines and snow-capped peaks, it offers a picturesque backdrop for fishing and kayaking.

HEART LAKE, aptly named for its heart-shaped outline, lies tucked away in the park's southern region. Accessible via a scenic hiking trail, it enchants visitors with its peaceful beauty and surrounding meadows brimming with wildflowers.

ISA LAKE, straddling the Continental Divide, is a natural wonder. Its waters flow in two directions, contributing to two distinct watersheds, showcasing a fascinating hydrological phenomenon.

TROUT LAKE, with its clear waters teeming with fish, is a popular spot for anglers and nature lovers alike. Surrounded by lush meadows and forests, it offers a serene retreat from the hustle and bustle of daily life.

DELUSION LAKE AND RIDDLE LAKE add an air of mystery to the park's landscape, their names evoking curiosity and inspiring the imagination of those who visit their shores.

Smaller lakes like Wrangler Lake, Grebe Lake, and Mallard Lake pepper the park's landscape, providing additional opportunities for exploration and relaxation. Each possesses its own unique charm, from Grebe Lake's bustling birdlife to Mallard Lake's tranquil atmosphere.

YELLOWSTONE VALLEYS

Yellowstone's expansive valleys provide excellent habitats for diverse wildlife. For optimal opportunities to observe bears, wolves, bison, pronghorn, and various other species, explore Lamar and Hayden valleys. Labeled as the American Serengeti, this destination showcases some of the nation's most remarkable wildlife.

LAMAR VALLEY IN NORTHERN YELLOWSTONE

Situated in the park's northeastern corner, Lamar Valley, along the Lamar River, earns its moniker as America's Serengeti due to its abundant and easily observable populations of large animals. The area hosts renowned inhabitants such as the Junction Butte and Lamar Canyon wolf packs, attracting enthusiasts armed with spotting scopes hoping to witness these majestic canines in their element. Alongside wolves, the Lamar Valley is home to expansive herds of bison, pronghorn, badgers, grizzly bears, bald eagles, osprey, deer, and coyotes. Numerous pullouts line the road, facilitating wildlife observation, with visitors encouraged to utilize the nearest one upon spotting any active wildlife.

A grizzly bear in Lamar Valley within Yellowstone. NPS Neal Herbert

For those able to divert their attention from the wildlife, the Lamar Valley offers various points of interest. Two modest, primitive campgrounds—*Slough Creek* and *Pebble Creek*—serve as ideal bases for early-rising wildlife enthusiasts. Yellowstone Forever's Lamar Buffalo Ranch accommodates students participating in the association's diverse field programs. Soda Butte, a remnant of a hot spring cone, sits just off the road on the valley's east side. Additionally, Trout Lake, accessible via a short hike from the road, provides an opportunity to stretch your legs and enjoy the surroundings. | **DIRECTIONS:** To reach Lamar Valley from Mammoth Hot Springs, follow Grand Loop Road east past Tower-Roosevelt, then continue on the Northeast Entrance road. From Cooke City and Silver Gate, enter the park via the Northeast Entrance and proceed westward.

HAYDEN VALLEY IN CENTRAL YELLOWSTONE

Hayden Valley, situated in Central Yellowstone, is renowned for its bustling population of bison. This expansive valley, located just north of the Lake area and Mud Volcano thermal area, serves as a prime habitat for these iconic creatures. Visitors frequently witness herds of bison leisurely grazing and congregating along the wide Yellowstone River that meanders through the valley. Additionally, Hayden Valley offers ample opportunities to spot other wildlife such as coyotes, waterfowl, grizzly bears, and wolves. *To maximize wildlife sightings*, you can utilize the various pullouts and overlooks along the park road or embark on the Mary Mountain Trail, stretching 21 miles from Hayden Valley to the Madison area, offering a chance to observe animals in their natural wilderness. *For optimal wildlife viewing*, it's advisable to plan outings during the dawn and dusk hours when animals are most active. Early risers should aim to reach the valleys before sunrise for the best chances of spotting wildlife. Hayden Valley shines particularly during the spring through fall seasons when park roads are open, although Lamar Valley remains accessible year-round by vehicle.

PELICAN VALLEY IN CENTRAL YELLOWSTONE

Pelican Valley in Yellowstone National Park is a wildlife-rich area east of Yellowstone Lake and southeast of Hayden Valley, known for its tranquil beauty and abundant wildlife. It is particularly famous for its bison population, with herds often seen grazing and roaming the valley floor, and sometimes crossing Pelican Creek. The valley also hosts elk, coyotes, grizzly bears, wolves, and various bird species, making it a paradise for wildlife enthusiasts and birdwatchers.

VIEWING TIPS

Timing: Visit early morning or late afternoon when wildlife is most active. | **Locations:** Scenic pullouts and overlooks provide good vantage points, and hiking the Pelican Valley Trail offers closer encounters. | **Seasonality:** *Spring:* Newborn wildlife appears. | *Summer:* The valley is lush with greenery and wildflowers. | *Fall:* Vibrant foliage colors the landscape, ideal for photography. | *Winter:* Snow-covered tranquility offers a serene backdrop for wildlife viewing.

Overall, Pelican Valley offers year-round wildlife experiences in a serene and pristine wilderness setting.

Bison moving at sunrise in Lamar Valley within Yellowstone
PHOTO: NPS/JACOB W FRANK

WILDLIFE WATCHING

MOOSE: Easily identifiable by their long snouts, bulbous noses, and dewlaps under their throats, moose stand out among other hoofed animals. Keep an eye out for them in areas abundant with willows. | **Place & Time to See Them:** In Yellowstone, moose can be spotted in Willow Park, Yellowstone Lake, Fishing Bridge, West Thumb, and Hayden Valley. In Grand Teton, they frequent Oxbow Bend, Blacktail Ponds, Mormon Row, and Antelope Flats Road.

BLACK BEAR: These omnivorous mammals can weigh up to 400 pounds and reach heights of two to four feet. Their fur coloration varies from black to blond or brown, occasionally leading visitors to mistake them for grizzlies. Throughout summer and fall, they migrate to higher elevations in pursuit of berries and trout. During winter, they hibernate, emerging in summer to mate. | **Place & Time to See Them:** Black bears are not visible during winter months due to hibernation, typically resurfacing in late February.

GRIZZLY BEAR: Distinguished by a prominent hump between their shoulders, blonde-tipped fur, long snout, and smaller ears compared to black bears, grizzlies, or "brown bears," are iconic Yellowstone residents. Their front claws measure between 2-4 inches, while black bears' claws range from 1-2 inches. Approximately 700 grizzlies inhabit the Yellowstone region. | **Place & Time to See Them:** Grizzlies are dormant during winter, hibernating until mid-to-late March, making them absent from winter sightings.

BISON: In 1916, the once thriving population of America's wild bison, totaling 60 million, had dwindled to a mere 23 animals. Today, Yellowstone's bison population stands at approximately 5,500, descendants of those resilient survivors. Weighing up to 2,000 pounds, bison may appear docile, but they are unpredictable and have caused injuries to visitors who approach them. | **Place & Time to See Them:** Encounter bison in Yellowstone's Lamar, Hayden, and Pelican valleys. In Grand Teton, observe them along the Snake River from Jackson Lake Dam south to Moose, Wyoming.

ELK: During summer, Yellowstone is home to around 10,000-20,000 elk, a number that decreases to 5,000 in winter. Many elk seek refuge in the National Elk Refuge in Jackson, Wyoming, during the colder months. Adult bull elk can weigh up to 700 pounds, while adult females may weigh up to 500 pounds. | **Place & Time to See Them:** Spot elk in Yellowstone at Mammoth Hot Springs, Lamar Valley, Norris Junction, Gibbon River, and Madison Junction. In Grand Teton, find them along Teton Park Road, Willow Flats, and around Two Ocean and Emma Mathilde lakes.

WOLF: Approximately 80 wolves roam in 10 packs within and around Yellowstone, contributing to about 450 wolves in the greater Yellowstone area. These highly social animals hunt elk, deer, and bison. In 1995, the reintroduction of 14 wolves from Canada marked a significant milestone in wolf conservation efforts. | **Place & Time to See Them:** Witness wolf packs in Yellowstone's Lamar Valley, Hayden Valley, Canyon area, and Blacktail Deer Plateau. The best times for viewing are dawn and dusk. In Grand Teton, catch a glimpse of them in Willow Flats.

TIPS FOR SPOTTING WILDLIFE

1. EQUIP YOURSELF: Pack binoculars or a spotting scope to enhance your wildlife viewing experience, as many animals may be challenging to spot with the naked eye alone.

2. FOLLOW THE CROWDS: In the Lamar Valley, keep an eye out for groups of people pulled over along the roadside; chances are high that someone has already spotted noteworthy wildlife such as wolves, bison, or other animals.

3. PRACTICE PATIENCE: Find a suitable vantage point and settle in quietly, allowing yourself to blend into the surroundings. By remaining still, you increase the likelihood of wildlife wandering into view without disturbance.

HIKING

DAY HIKES IN THE CANYON AREA OF
YELLOWSTONE NATIONAL PARK

The Canyon Area of Yellowstone National Park offers a diverse range of day hikes that cater to different skill levels and interests. From serene lake trails to challenging mountain ascents, hikers can experience the park's breathtaking landscapes, abundant wildlife, and inspirational vistas.

1. CASCADE LAKE TRAIL: This trail takes hikers through open meadows to Cascade Lake, where wildflowers bloom and wildlife sightings are common. The hike offers a tranquil experience surrounded by yellow grass, green trees, and forested mountains. | *Location:* Canyon Village | *Duration:* 2–3 Hours | *Season:* Summer, Fall

2. CHITTENDEN ROAD - MOUNT WASHBURN TRAIL: The shortest route to the top of Mount Washburn, this trail provides panoramic views and interpretive exhibits. Wildflowers adorn the alpine meadows, making the ascent visually rewarding. | *Location:* Canyon Village | *Duration:* 3–5 Hours | *Season:* Summer, FallDunraven Pass

3. MOUNT WASHBURN TRAIL: Starting at Dunraven Pass, this trail ascends Mount Washburn, offering spectacular views along the way. Note that the trailhead parking lot at Dunraven Pass may be closed for improvements during certain times. | *Location:* Canyon Village | *Duration:* 3–6 Hours | *Season:* Summer, Fall

4. GREBE LAKE TRAIL: This trail follows an old fire road through meadows and forests, some of which were affected by the fires of 1988. The hike leads to Grebe Lake, nestled at the base of forested slopes. | *Location:* Canyon Village | *Duration:* 3–4 Hours | *Season:* Summer, Fall

5. HOWARD EATON TRAIL (CANYON AREA): This versatile trail passes by four lakes and traverses through forests, meadows, and marshes. Hikers can choose their destination, making it a flexible option for different hiking preferences. | *Location:* Canyon Village |

Duration: 5–6 Hours | *Season:* Summer, Fall

6. MOUNT WASHBURN SPUR TRAIL: A longer hike that begins at the Grand Canyon of the Yellowstone and ascends the east side of Mount Washburn. This trail is suited for experienced hikers seeking a full-day adventure. | *Location:* Grand Canyon of the Yellowstone River | *Duration:* 8–10 Hours | **Season:** Summer, Fall

7. OBSERVATION PEAK TRAIL: Hike to the top of Observation Peak for a stunning view of the Yellowstone wilderness. This trail offers a challenging climb with a rewarding view at the summit. | *Location:* Canyon Village | *Duration:* 5–6 Hours | *Season:* Summer, Fall

8. RIBBON LAKE TRAIL: A scenic hike to Ribbon Lake, passing by Lily Pad and Clear lakes. The trail is ideal for those seeking a moderate hike with beautiful lake views. | *Location:* Grand Canyon of the Yellowstone River | *Duration:* 3–4 Hours | *Season:* Summer, Fall

9. SEVEN MILE HOLE TRAIL: This trail offers dramatic views along the rim of the Grand Canyon of the Yellowstone, including the Silver Cord Cascade. It then descends to Seven Mile Hole, providing an immersive canyon experience. | *Location:* Grand Canyon of the Yellowstone River | *Duration:* 5–8 Hours | **Season:** Summer, Fall

DAY HIKES IN THE LAKE & FISHING BRIDGE AREA OF YELLOWSTONE NATIONAL PARK

The Lake and Fishing Bridge area of Yellowstone National Park offers a variety of day hikes that provide stunning views, encounters with diverse wildlife, and unique geological features. These trails are suitable for different levels of hiking experience and provide a mix of serene lake views, challenging mountain ascents, and fascinating geothermal activity.

10. AVALANCHE PEAK TRAIL: Known as one of the most strenuous day hikes in the park, the Avalanche Peak Trail rewards hikers with breathtaking views of Yellowstone's tallest and most remote alpine peaks. The climb is challenging but the panoramic views from the summit are worth the effort. | **Location:** Yellowstone Lake | *Duration:* 3–4 Hours | *Season:* Summer, Fall

11. ELEPHANT BACK MOUNTAIN TRAIL: This trail ascends Elephant Back Mountain, offering panoramic views of Yellowstone Lake and the surrounding forested landscape. It's a moderate hike that provides a spectacular vantage point of the area. | *Location:* Lake Village | *Duration:* 2–3 Hours | *Season:* Summer, Fall

12. MUD VOLCANO TRAIL: A loop trail that guides hikers through the otherworldly Mud Volcano area. Encounter bubbling mudpots, steam-cooked trees, and unusual odors in this geothermal hotspot. The bizarre landscape offers a unique and memorable hiking experience. | *Location:* Mud Volcano | *Duration:* 1–2 Hours | *Season:* Winter, Spring, Summer, Fall

13. NATURAL BRIDGE TRAIL: This hike takes you through a forest and along an old service road to a natural bridge formed from rhyolite rock by Bridge Creek. It's a relatively easy hike with a rewarding view of the natural rock formation. | *Location:* Bridge Bay Marina | *Duration:* 1–2 Hours | *Season:* Summer, Fall

14. PELICAN CREEK NATURE TRAIL: A short loop trail that introduces hikers to a variety of Yellowstone habitats. The trail winds through a forest to the shore of Yellowstone Lake, offering opportunities to spot diverse bird species and enjoy scenic lake views. | *Location:* Yellowstone Lake | *Duration:* 30–60 Minutes | *Season:* Summer, Fall

15. PELICAN VALLEY TRAIL: This trail takes hikers through forests, meadows, and a river valley, making it one of the best areas in the lower 48 states for observing grizzly bears. The hike offers a chance to experience Yellowstone's wild and pristine natural environment. *Location:* Fishing Bridge | *Duration:* 3–4 Hours | *Season:* Summer, Fall

16. STORM POINT TRAIL: The trail passes by Indian Pond and through a forest to the shores of Yellowstone Lake. Look for marmots in the rocky areas near Storm Point, and enjoy the serene beauty of the lake and surrounding landscape. | *Location:* Fishing Bridge | *Duration:* 1–2 Hours | *Season:* Summer, Fall

DAY HIKES IN THE MADISON AREA OF

YELLOWSTONE NATIONAL PARK

The Madison area of Yellowstone National Park offers a variety of day hikes that traverse through dense forests and provide stunning views of lakes and mountains. These trails are perfect for those seeking a mix of short, easy hikes and more challenging treks.

17. HARLEQUIN LAKE TRAIL: This gentle, uphill trail meanders through a dense conifer forest leading to a small, picturesque lake dotted with lily pads at the base of a sloping cliff. It's a short and easy hike, perfect for families and those looking for a quick nature escape. | *Location:* Madison Junction | *Duration:* 30–60 Minutes | *Season:* Spring, Summer, Fall

18. PURPLE MOUNTAIN TRAIL: These hikes in the Madison area are ideal for experiencing the natural beauty and serenity of Yellowstone National Park. The Harlequin Lake Trail offers a brief, peaceful walk to a scenic lake, while the Purple Mountain Trail provides a more vigorous hike with breathtaking panoramic views. Always check trail conditions and weather forecasts before setting out on your hike. | *Location:* Madison Junction | *Duration:* 3–5 Hours | *Season:* Summer, Fall

DAY HIKES IN THE MAMMOTH AREA OF YELLOWSTONE NATIONAL PARK

The Mammoth Area of Yellowstone National Park offers a variety of day hikes that showcase the region's diverse landscapes, including forests, meadows, geothermal features, and panoramic mountain views. These trails cater to different hiking preferences, from short, easy walks to more challenging climbs.

19. BEAVER PONDS TRAIL: This trail winds through forests, sagebrush meadows, and stands of Douglas-fir and aspen. Hikers may spot beavers, muskrats, and water birds around the beaver ponds. It's a moderate hike with varied terrain and wildlife viewing opportunities. | *Location:* Mammoth Hot Springs | *Duration:* 2–5 Hours | *Season:* Winter, Spring, Summer, Fall

20. BLACKTAIL DEER CREEK TO YELLOWSTONE RIVER TRAIL:

Follow Blacktail Deer Creek through rolling grassy hills and Douglas-fir forests to a suspension bridge over the Yellowstone River. This scenic trail offers a mix of open fields and wooded areas, making it a diverse hiking experience. | **_Location:_** East of Mammoth Hot Springs | **_Duration:_** 4–5 Hours | **_Season:_** Spring, Summer, Fall

21. BUNSEN PEAK TRAIL: Ascend to the top of Bunsen Peak for panoramic views of Swan Lake Flats, the Gallatin Mountain Range, and the Mammoth Hot Springs area. This moderately strenuous hike rewards hikers with stunning vistas and a sense of accomplishment. | **_Location:_** Mammoth Hot Springs | **_Duration_**: 2–3 Hours | **_Season:_** Summer, Fall

22. FORCES OF THE NORTHERN RANGE SELF-GUIDED TRAIL: This self-guided trail along a boardwalk winds through the grasslands of Yellowstone's northern range. It provides educational exhibits about the park's ecosystem and geological forces, making it an informative and easy walk.
Location: East of Mammoth Hot Springs | Duration: 30–60 Minutes | Season: Spring, Summer, Fall

23. LAVA CREEK TRAIL: Follow Lava Creek, passing by the picturesque Undine Falls and the junction with the Gardner River. This trail offers scenic views and is suitable for a moderate hike through diverse landscapes. | **_Location:_** Mammoth Hot Springs | **_Duration:_** 2–3 Hours | **_Season:_** Winter, Spring, Summer, Fall

24. MAMMOTH HOT SPRINGS TRAILS: Explore the large travertine terraces formed by ever-shifting hot springs. This series of short trails & boardwalks provide an up-close look at one of Yellowstone's most famous geothermal areas. | **_Location:_** Mammoth Hot Springs | **_Duration:_** 30–90 Minutes | **_Season:_** Winter, Spring, Summer, Fall

25. OSPREY FALLS TRAIL: Walk along an old service road through meadows before descending into one of the deepest canyons in the park to see Osprey Falls, which plunges over the edge of an old lava flow. This hike is moderately strenuous but offers a spectacular waterfall view. | **_Location:_** Mammoth Hot Springs | **_Duration:_** 4–6

Hours | *Season:* Summer, Fall

26. RESCUE CREEK TRAIL: This trail gradually climbs through aspens and meadows, then descends through forests to sagebrush flats leading to a footbridge across the Gardner River. It's a moderate hike that showcases a variety of ecosystems. | **Location:** Mammoth Hot Springs | **Duration:** 4–6 Hours | **Season:** Winter, Spring, Summer, Fall

27. SEPULCHER MOUNTAIN TRAIL: Climb to the summit of Sepulcher Mountain while keeping an eye out for mountain goats, bighorn sheep, and moose. This challenging hike provides rewarding views from the rocky summit and opportunities for wildlife sightings. | **Location:** Mammoth Hot Springs | **Duration:** 6–8 Hours | **Season:** Summer, Fall

28. WRAITH FALLS TRAIL: Cross sagebrush meadows, marshland, and mixed conifer forest to the base of Wraith Falls on Lupine Creek. This short and easy hike leads to a scenic waterfall and is suitable for all ages. | **Location:** Mammoth Hot Springs | **Duration:** 30–60 Minutes | **Season:** Winter, Spring, Summer, Fall

DAY HIKES IN THE OLD FAITHFUL AREA OF YELLOWSTONE NATIONAL PARK

The Old Faithful Area in Yellowstone National Park offers a diverse range of day hikes that highlight the park's geothermal wonders, beautiful waterfalls, and scenic vistas. Here are some notable trails:

29. FAIRY FALLS TRAIL: This trail takes you to one of Yellowstone's most spectacular waterfalls, Fairy Falls. The hike offers stunning views of the Grand Prismatic Spring along the way, making it a popular choice for visitors. | *Location:* Midway Geyser Basin | *Duration:* 3–5 Hours | *Season:* Winter, Summer, Fall

30. HOWARD EATON TRAIL (OLD FAITHFUL AREA): Hike up a burned hill and continue through a spruce-fir forest to reach Lone Star Geyser, where you can witness the geyser erupting every three hours. This trail offers a mix of forested and open landscapes. | *Location:* Upper Geyser Basin | *Duration:* 3–5 Hours | *Season:* Winter,

Summer, Fall

31. SENTINEL MEADOWS & QUEEN'S LAUNDRY TRAIL: Follow the Firehole River through meadows to a hydrothermal area. This trail features large sinter mounds from hot springs and the remnants of an old, incomplete bathhouse, providing a unique glimpse into Yellowstone's geothermal activity. | _**Location:**_ Midway Geyser Basin | _**Duration:**_ 2–4 Hours | _**Season:**_ Winter, Summer, Fall

32. GRAND PRISMATIC OVERLOOK TRAIL: A short but rewarding hike that takes you to an overlook of the Grand Prismatic Spring, offering an aerial view of its vivid colors and expansive size. | _**Location:**_ Midway Geyser Basin | _**Duration:**_ 1–2 Hours | _**Season:**_ Winter, Summer, Fall

33. LONE STAR GEYSER TRAIL: This pleasant, partially paved trail follows the Firehole River to Lone Star Geyser. The geyser erupts every three hours, creating a spectacular display of steam and water. _**Location:**_ Upper Geyser Basin | _**Duration:**_ 2–3 Hours | _**Season:**_ Winter, Summer, Fall

34. MALLARD LAKE TRAIL: Cross the Firehole River & pass by Pipeline Hot Springs before climbing through rolling hills of lodgepole pine and open, rocky areas to reach Mallard Lake. The trail offers diverse scenery and a peaceful destination at the lake. | _**Location:**_ Upper Geyser Basin | _**Duration:**_ 3–6 Hours | _**Season:**_ Winter, Summer, Fall

35. MYSTIC FALLS TRAIL: Follow a creek through a mixed conifer forest to Mystic Falls, where the Little Firehole River drops from the Madison Plateau. This scenic hike provides beautiful views of the waterfall and surrounding landscape. | _**Location:**_ Upper Geyser Basin | _**Duration:**_ 2–4 Hours | _**Season:**_ Winter, Summer, Fall

36. OBSERVATION POINT TRAIL: A short hike to a viewpoint that offers panoramic views of the Upper Geyser Basin, including Old Faithful. This trail is perfect for those looking for a quick but rewarding hike with excellent photo opportunities. | _**Location:**_ Upper Geyser Basin | _**Duration:**_ 1–3 Hours | _**Season:**_ Winter, Spring, Summer,

Fall

These trails in the Old Faithful Area provide a range of hiking experiences, from easy walks to more challenging treks, each showcasing the unique geothermal and natural beauty of Yellowstone National Park. Be sure to stay on designated trails to protect the fragile environment and for your safety.

SCENIC DRIVES

Exploring Yellowstone National Park is best done via its scenic drives, which reveal its vast and varied landscapes. These routes traverse through alpine lakes, evergreen forests, majestic peaks, and natural wonders. Expect to see steaming geysers, bubbling hot springs, and freely roaming wildlife. Here are some of the best scenic drives to enjoy:

GRAND LOOP ROAD

The Grand Loop Road, a 142-mile scenic route forming a figure eight through Yellowstone, passes the park's major attractions. Boardwalks and trails lead to highlights like the travertine terraces of Mammoth Hot Springs and the diverse geysers in Norris Geyser Basin. You can marvel at the vibrant Grand Prismatic Spring and the renowned Old Faithful. The loop continues to Yellowstone Lake, one of North America's highest and largest lakes. Explore the Mud Volcano Trail and listen for the waterfalls at the Grand Canyon of Yellowstone. This route connects to the Beartooth Highway, one of America's most scenic drives. Plan for four to seven hours to complete the loop, depending on traffic.

Highlights: Mammoth Hot Springs, Norris Geyser Basin, Grand Prismatic Spring, Old Faithful, Yellowstone Lake, Mud Volcano Trail, Grand Canyon of the Yellowstone | **Time Required:** 4-7 hours, depending on traffic and stops.

BEARTOOTH HIGHWAY (US 212)

The Beartooth Highway (US 212) is a breathtaking route through Yellowstone, winding through the Absaroka-Beartooth Wilderness along the Montana and Wyoming border. At 11,000 feet, Beartooth Pass offers panoramic views of ponds, alpine lakes, and snow-capped peaks. Key stops include the pyramid-shaped peak rising from granite mountains, Beartooth Lake, and the historic Top of The World Store. Without stops, the drive takes about 4.5 hours. Note that this route is closed from mid-October to late May but is accessible to snowmobiles in winter. | **FEATURES:** *Beartooth Lake:* Ideal for fishing and kayaking. | *Top of The World Store:* Historic stop with unique views. | *Time Required:* 4.5 hours without stops. | *Accessibility:* Closed from mid-October to late May; open to snowmobiles in winter.

CHIEF JOSEPH SCENIC HIGHWAY (US 296)

The 62-mile Chief Joseph Scenic Highway (US 296) stretches between Cody, Wyoming, and the Beartooth Highway, meandering through the Shoshone National Forest and the wild Clarks Fork of the Yellowstone River. A notable stop is Dead Indian Pass, where you can hike to see an impressive granite gorge and waterfall. This route is maintained year-round and takes about an hour to drive.

HIGHLIGHTS: Dead Indian Pass: Viewpoint with a trail to a granite gorge and waterfall. | Time Required: 1 hour.

BUFFALO BILL SCENIC BYWAY (US 14)

The Buffalo Bill Scenic Byway (US 14) covers 27.5 miles from Cody, WY, through the Wapiti Valley and North Fork of the Shoshone River to Yellowstone's east entrance. This route showcases the volcanic Absaroka Mountains and Yellowstone's diverse wildlife. The Buffalo Bill Reservoir is a scenic spot for a lunch break. Key points of interest include Colter's Hell, Mummy Cave, and Pahaska Tepee, all on the National Register of Historic Places. | **HIGHLIGHTS:** *Buffalo Bill Reservoir:* Scenic spot for a picnic. | *Colter's Hell, Mummy Cave, Pahaska Tepee:* Historic sites listed on the National Register of Historic Places. | *Time Required:* Varies, depending on stops.

GALLATIN VALLEY ROUTE (US 191)

The Gallatin Valley Route (US 191) follows the Gallatin River through tranquil valleys, featured in the film *A River Runs Through It*. This less-crowded route dates back to the days of Lewis and Clark. It's a scenic alternative to the main park loops, offering a peaceful drive through the Madison and Gallatin mountain ranges. | **HIGHLIGHTS:** *A River Runs Through It:* Scenic spot from the film. | *Lewis and Clark Expedition Route:* Historical significance. | *Time Required:* Less crowded and tranquil, perfect for a leisurely drive.

PARADISE VALLEY ROUTE (US 89)

The Paradise Valley Route (US 89) follows the Yellowstone River through the Gallatin and Absaroka Mountain Ranges, passing through Yankee Jim Canyon, known for its white-water rafting. The alternative East River Road offers broad valleys and ranchlands alongside the Yellowstone River. | **HIGHLIGHTS:** *Yankee Jim Canyon:* prime spot for white-water rafting. | *East River Road:* Alternative scenic route through ranchlands and valleys. | *Time Required:* Varies, offering stunning views and tranquility.

SCENIC DRIVES IN NORTH YELLOWSTONE

GARDINER TO COOKE CITY – 52 MI (84 KM)

This drive begins at the North Entrance Station in Gardiner, Montana, and extends to the Northeast Entrance at Silver Gate and Cooke City. It's the only road open year-round to private vehicles, though snowstorms can cause temporary closures. Starting from Gardiner, the road passes under the Roosevelt Arch, crosses the 45th Parallel, and reaches Mammoth Hot Springs. Key stops include Undine Falls and the Petrified Tree. From Tower Junction, the route traverses the wildlife-rich Lamar Valley before climbing into the Absaroka Mountains, ending in Cooke City.

UPPER GRAND LOOP ROAD – 70 MI (113 KM)

Connecting Mammoth Hot Springs with Norris Geyser Basin, Canyon Village, and Tower-Roosevelt, this loop showcases a range of geothermal and scenic wonders. Highlights include the hoodoos of Terrace Mountain, Swan Lake Flat for wildlife spotting, and the geological marvel of Obsidian Cliff. Stops at Roaring Mountain and the Norris Geyser Basin provide insight into Yellowstone's volcanic activity.

SCENIC DRIVES IN OLD FAITHFUL AND WEST YELLOWSTONE

WEST ENTRANCE ROAD – 14 MI (22.5 KM)

This road from West Yellowstone to Madison Junction is perfect for evening wildlife-watching. It follows the Madison River, with ample opportunities to see bison, elk, and even bobcats. The meadows along the route are particularly rich with wildlife during the summer and fall.

LOWER GRAND LOOP ROAD – 96 MI (154 KM)

Linking Madison, Norris, Canyon Village, West Thumb, and Old Faithful, this loop offers extensive wildlife watching and visits to major attractions like the Grand Canyon of the Yellowstone and Old Faithful. The route passes through diverse landscapes, including geyser basins, meadows, and lakeshores.

GEYSER BASIN TOUR – 16 MI (26 KM)

From Madison Junction to Old Faithful, this drive follows the Firehole River and provides access to several major geyser basins. Highlights include Fountain Paint Pot, Firehole Lake, and the Old Faithful complex. The road also features short scenic detours like Firehole Canyon Drive, known for Firehole Falls, and Firehole Lake Drive, which showcases thermal features like Great Fountain Geyser.

SCENIC DRIVES IN CANYON & LAKE COUNTRY

South Entrance Road – 22 MI (35 KM)

Connecting the South Entrance with Grant Village and West Thumb, this forested road runs along the Lewis River and past Lewis Falls and Lewis Lake, offering serene views and photo opportunities.

EAST ENTRANCE ROAD – 27 MI (43 KM)

From the East Entrance Station, this road climbs through dramatic cliffs and offers panoramic views, particularly at Sylvan Pass. Key stops include Sylvan Lake and the Lake Butte Overlook, which provides sweeping views of Yellowstone Lake and the Absaroka Mountains.

HAYDEN VALLEY DRIVE

From Canyon Village to Fishing Bridge, this segment of the Lower Grand Loop Road passes through the wildlife-rich Hayden Valley.

Early morning or dusk drives here often yield sightings of bison, elk, and sometimes bears or wolves. The route also features geothermal sites like Mud Volcano and Sulphur Cauldron.

PRACTICAL TIPS FOR SCENIC DRIVES

Timing: Plan your trip around Yellowstone's scenic drives, open from late spring to early fall. Check road conditions, opening dates, and winter restrictions before visiting. | **Wildlife Watching:** Dawn and dusk are ideal for spotting wildlife. Drive slowly and expect possible animal-related traffic jams. | **Safety:** Use second gear on steep descents to prevent overheating brakes. Be aware of bear activity and potential road closures. Carry a map, extra water, and emergency supplies as cell service is limited. | **Respect Nature:** Follow Leave No Trace principles to preserve the park's beauty.

Yellowstone's scenic drives offer an unforgettable way to explore the park's natural splendor, from geothermal wonders to majestic mountains. Enjoy your journey!

BOATING, KAYAKING & FISHING

Yellowstone National Park offers a variety of water adventures, from boating and paddling to fishing and kayaking, allowing visitors to experience the park's stunning waterways up close.

BOAT TOURS OF YELLOWSTONE LAKE

One of the best ways to explore the vast Yellowstone Lake, the largest high-elevation lake in the Lower 48 states, is by taking a boat tour aboard the Lake Queen. Departing from Bridge Bay Marina, these tours navigate the lake's 136 square miles and provide an engaging way to learn about the area's history, including the iconic Lake Yellowstone Hotel, built in 1891. Tour participants often see eagles, ospreys, and even bison along the shores. Tours run from mid-June through mid-August, with multiple departures throughout the day. Advance booking is recommended, and you can reserve your spot by calling *307-344-7311* or visiting the Yellowstone National Park Lodges website at *https://www.yellowstonenationalparklodges.com/adventures/water-adventures*

BOATING IN YELLOWSTONE

If you are looking to explore on your own, motorboats and rowboats are available for rent at Bridge Bay Marina. Yellowstone Lake and Lewis Lake are perfect for cruising and fishing, with certain zones designated for non-motorized boating only. A boat permit is required, costing $10 per week, which can be purchased at the South Entrance, Bridge Bay Ranger Station, or Grant Village Backcountry Office. More information on rentals and boating guidelines can be found on the Yellowstone National Park Lodges website at *https://www.yellowstonenationalparklodges.com/adventures/water-adventures*

PADDLING ON YELLOWSTONE'S LAKES

For a more tranquil experience, paddling a kayak or canoe on Yellowstone's lakes offers a serene escape from shoreline crowds. Yellowstone Lake, with its numerous remote campsites, and Shoshone Lake, the largest backcountry lake in the Lower 48

accessible only by paddle via the Lewis River, are ideal destinations. A weekly boat permit for non-motorized vessels costs $5 and can be purchased at the same locations as motorboat permits. While there are no rentals within the park, outfitters like _Geyser Kayak Tours_ (**Website:** _https://geyserkayak.com_ | **Phone Number:** _+1 307-413-6177_ and _Yellowstone Hiking Guides_ offer guided trips. | **Address:** 1079 US-287, Cameron, MT 59720, USA | **Website:** _https:// www.yellowstonehikingguides.com_ |
Phone Number: _+1 406-848-1144_

FISHING IN YELLOWSTONE

Yellowstone is a fishing paradise with miles of rivers and streams, as well as tranquil lakes, providing excellent opportunities for anglers. The Madison River is known for its brown and rainbow trout, while Yellowstone Lake is home to native cutthroat trout. The Gardner River offers a mix of brookies, rainbow, and brown trout. A national park fishing license is required for anglers aged 16 and up, with fees set at $18 for 3 days, $25 for a week, or $40 for a season pass. For more detailed information on fishing locations and regulations, you should refer to the park's guidelines.

Yellowstone National Park's diverse water activities provide an array of ways to enjoy its natural beauty, whether you're interested in a guided boat tour, a quiet paddle, or the thrill of fishing in pristine waters.

CAMPING

Camping in Yellowstone National Park offers a variety of experiences, whether you prefer the convenience of an RV park with full hookups or the tranquility of a primitive campsite. The park features 12 campgrounds with over 2,000 established campsites, most of which require reservations well in advance due to high demand.

CAR CAMPING REGULATIONS: Car camping or overnight vehicle parking is strictly regulated to maintain the park's natural beauty and wildlife safety. Camping is only allowed in designated campgrounds, not in pullouts, parking areas, picnic grounds, or any unauthorized areas.

YELLOWSTONE CAMPGROUNDS

1. BRIDGE BAY CAMPGROUND: Situated at an elevation of 7,800 feet (2,377 meters), is located near Yellowstone Lake, which is one of the largest high-altitude freshwater lakes in North America. You can enjoy stunning views of the lake and the Absaroka Range that rises above its eastern shore. Reservations for this campground are managed by Yellowstone National Park Lodges. | **Fee:** $33 + taxes | **Sites:** 431 | **Amenities:** Seasonal potable water, dump station, amphitheater, food storage lockers, and more. Notable for its stunning views of Yellowstone Lake & the Absaroka Range.

2. CANYON CAMPGROUND: Located at an elevation of 7,900 feet (2,408 meters), is nestled in a lodgepole pine forest at Canyon Village. It is situated south of the Washburn range and close to the stunning Grand Canyon of the Yellowstone River. Canyon Village features stores, restaurants, and lodging. Nearby hiking trails include Cascade Lake, Mount Washburn, and the Canyon Rim trails. Reservations for this campground are handled by Yellowstone National Park Lodges. | **Fee:** $39 + taxes | **Sites:** 272 | **Amenities:** Potable water, dump station, showers & amphitheater. Located near the Grand Canyon of the Yellowstone River, offering numerous hiking trails

3. FISHING BRIDGE RV PARK: Situated at an elevation of 7,800 feet (2,377 meters), is near the Yellowstone River where it flows out of Yellowstone Lake towards the Grand Canyon of the Yellowstone. It is the only campground in Yellowstone that offers water, sewer, and electrical hookups. Due to frequent grizzly bear activity in the area, tents and tent campers are not permitted. Reservations for this campground are managed by Yellowstone National Park Lodges. | **Fee:** $89/$99 + taxes | **Sites:** 310 | **Amenities:** Full hookups, dump station, laundry, and staff on site. The only campground in Yellowstone with water, sewer, and electrical hookups. No tents allowed due to bear activity.

4. GRANT VILLAGE CAMPGROUND: Situated at an elevation of 7,800 feet (2,377 meters), is located in Grant Village, near the Grand Loop Road at the southern end of Yellowstone Lake. It is one of the park's larger campgrounds, offering group and wheelchair-accessible sites. Nearby amenities include stores, a restaurant, a gas station, a visitor center, and a boat ramp. Reservations for this campground are managed by Yellowstone National Park Lodges. | **Fee:** $39 + taxes | **Sites:** 429 | **Amenities:** Potable water, dump station, amphitheater, and food storage lockers. Close to stores, a restaurant, and a visitor center.

5. MADISON CAMPGROUND: Located at an elevation of 6,800 feet (2,073 meters), is approximately 14 miles east of the town of West Yellowstone and 16 miles north of Old Faithful. Nearby, the Gibbon and Firehole rivers merge to form the Madison River. In early summer, the meadows are filled with wildflowers and bison, and in September and October, the bugling of elk can often be heard. Reservations for this campground are managed by Yellowstone National Park Lodges. | **Fee:** $33 + taxes | **Sites:** 276 | **Amenities:** Potable water, dump station, and amphitheater. Near the confluence of the Gibbon and Firehole rivers, great for wildlife viewing.

RESERVABLE THROUGH RECREATION.GOV

1. INDIAN CREEK CAMPGROUND: Indian Creek Campground, at an elevation of 7,300 feet (2,225 meters), is located about eight miles south of Mammoth Hot Springs on the road to Norris. Situated near the base of the Gallatin Mountains, it offers stunning views of Electric Peak. The area provides easy access to fishing and hiking. Being set away from the main road, this campground offers a quieter and more primitive experience compared to many other locations. Reservations for this campground are managed by the National Park Service. | **Fee:** $20 | **Sites:** 70 | **Amenities:** Seasonal potable water and food storage lockers. Offers a quieter, more primitive camping experience.

2. LEWIS LAKE CAMPGROUND: Lewis Lake Campground, at an elevation of 7,800 feet (2,377 meters), is located about eight miles from the South Entrance and is a short walk from the southeast shore of Lewis Lake. A boat ramp is available near the campground information and registration area, and canoes, kayaks, and motor boats are permitted on Lewis Lake. Boat permits and an aquatic invasive species inspection by park staff are required. Reservations for this campground are managed by the National Park Service. | Fee: $20 | Sites: 84 | Amenities: Seasonal potable water and food storage lockers. Near Lewis Lake, popular for boating and fishing.

3. MAMMOTH CAMPGROUND: The only campground in the park open year-round, is situated at an elevation of 6,200 feet (1,890 meters) and is located five miles south of the park's North Entrance. Scattered juniper and Douglas fir trees provide shade during the hot summer months. The campground is conveniently close to fishing, hiking, and the Mammoth Hot Springs. It also offers excellent wildlife viewing opportunities, with elk and bison occasionally passing through the area. This campground, managed by the National Park Service, is reservable from April 1 to October 15. | **Fee:** $25 | **Sites:** 82 | **Amenities:** Year-round potable water, food storage lockers, and staff on site. Located near Mammoth Hot Springs with abundant wildlife.

4. SLOUGH CREEK CAMPGROUND: Located near some of the best wildlife watching opportunities in the park, is situated at the end of a two-mile dirt road. It is best suited for tents and small RVs. The area offers numerous hiking and fishing opportunities, including access to the Slough Creek Trail nearby. At night, campers can enjoy a quiet atmosphere with unobstructed views of the stars and the potential to hear wolves howl. The campground's elevation is 6,250 feet (1,905 meters). Reservations for this campground are managed by the NPS. | **Fee:** $20 | **Sites:** 16 | **Amenities:** Seasonal potable water and food storage lockers. Ideal for small RVs and tents, with excellent wildlife viewing opportunities.

TEMPORARILY CLOSED CAMPGROUNDS IN 2024

Norris Campground | Pebble Creek Campground | Tower Fall Campground

TIPS FOR CAMPERS

Reservations: Most campsites must be reserved in advance. It's best to book as early as possible to secure a spot. | **Accessibility:** Many campgrounds have accessible sites for individuals with disabilities. **Facilities:** Amenities vary by campground and can include potable water, dump stations, food storage lockers, and amphitheaters. | **Wildlife Safety:** Proper food storage is essential to avoid attracting bears and other wildlife.

CAMPGROUND TIPS & REGULATIONS

LIFETIME PASSES: To enter, lifetime pass holders must present their pass and identification. Lost or stolen pass information cannot be retrieved, and photos or receipts are not accepted. On snowmobiles, lifetime passes admit the signer(s), and on snowcoaches or shuttles, they allow entry for the signer and up to three additional adults. Children under 16 are free. | **SENIOR PASS ($80):** For U.S. citizens or permanent residents aged 62 or older. Covers entrance fees at national parks, wildlife refuges, and other federal lands. May provide a 50% discount on some amenities. Available online or at Yellowstone entrances. | **ACCESS PASS (FREE):** For U.S. citizens or permanent residents with a permanent disability. Covers entrance fees and may offer a 50% discount on some amenities. Requires additional documentation. Available online or at Yellowstone entrances. | **MILITARY VETERANS AND GOLD STAR FAMILY ACCESS PASS (FREE):** For Gold Star Families & U.S. military veterans. Covers entrance fees at national parks, wildlife refuges, and other federal lands. | **RVS:** Rental RVs or camper units from outside the park are not allowed for delivery or pickup. Fishing Bridge RV Park is the only campground with water, sewer, and electrical hookups (50 amp service) & is restricted to hard-sided vehicles only. Dump stations may close in freezing temperatures. | **GROUP CAMPSITES:** Available at Bridge Bay, Grant Village, and Madison campgrounds for large groups with a designated leader, such as educational groups. Fees range from $165 to $475 per night, depending on group size. Advance reservations are required through Yellowstone National Park Lodges.

PHOTOGRAPHY

With its diverse landscapes and abundant wildlife, Yellowstone is a paradise for photographers. Capture stunning images of the park's geothermal features, wildlife, and picturesque vistas. Yellowstone offers unparalleled opportunities to capture the wonders of nature. From the birth of a bison calf to the dramatic eruptions of geysers, every moment in the park is a potential masterpiece.

KEY GUIDELINES FOR SAFE AND RESPECTFUL PHOTOGRAPHY

While the allure of Yellowstone's natural beauty is irresistible, it is crucial to follow certain guidelines to protect both the park and its visitors:

1. ZOOM WITH YOUR LENS, NOT YOUR FEET: Approaching or pursuing wildlife is not only dangerous but can also provoke aggressive behavior from animals. Always maintain a distance of 100 yards (91 meters) from bears and wolves, and 25 yards (23 meters) from all other animals. Utilize zoom lenses with focal lengths up to 300 or 400mm for close-up shots without compromising safety.

2. STAY ON BOARDWALKS AND TRAILS IN THERMAL AREAS: The park's hot springs and geysers, though stunning, are perilous. Boiling water often lies just below the surface, making off-trail exploration extremely dangerous. Ensure tripod legs remain on boardwalks and allow space for others to pass safely.

3. PARK IN ROADSIDE PULLOUTS: To prevent traffic blockages, always park in designated roadside pullouts. Avoid driving or parking on roadside vegetation, and stay with your vehicle during heavy traffic to keep the roads clear.

4. CARRY BEAR SPRAY: Given that all of Yellowstone is bear habitat, carrying and knowing how to use bear spray is essential for safety. Familiarize yourself with other best practices for traveling safely in bear country.

5. LEAVE THE DRONE AT HOME: The use of unmanned aircraft is prohibited in Yellowstone, so plan your photography accordingly.

POPULAR PHOTOGRAPHIC SPOTS

Yellowstone's diverse scenery provides countless opportunities for stunning photography:

GRAND PRISMATIC SPRING: The largest hot spring in Yellowstone, known for its vibrant bacterial mats and azure pool, offers an otherworldly scene. The Fairy Falls Trailhead provides an elevated view, while the boardwalks in Midway Geyser Basin offer ground-level perspectives. Remember to stay on designated paths.

LOWER FALLS OF THE YELLOWSTONE RIVER: This iconic waterfall can be captured from various viewpoints like Brink of Lower Falls, Lookout Point, and Artist Point. On sunny days, a rainbow often forms in the spray below the falls.

OLD FAITHFUL: Timing is crucial to photograph this famous geyser. Check the park's Geyser Activity Page or call 307-344-2751 (option 2) for eruption predictions. Arrive early for a front-row seat, and be prepared for the geyser's peak height shortly after it starts erupting.

ADDITIONAL SUBJECTS AND LOCATIONS

LAMAR VALLEY: Known for its high concentration of wildlife, including bison and wolves, this area offers excellent opportunities for wildlife photography. Always remember to keep your distance and use a zoom lens.

UPPER GEYSER BASIN: Home to numerous geysers, including predictably erupting ones near Old Faithful. Spend time exploring the boardwalks and stop by the visitor education center for geyser eruption predictions.

LAKES AND RIVERS: Springtime transforms Yellowstone's water bodies, with melting snow swelling lakes & rivers, creating dramatic photographic opportunities. Many waterfalls, like Firehole, Gibbon, and Lewis Falls, can be easily accessed from roads or overlooks.

NIGHT SKIES AND HOT SPRINGS: Clear nights reveal star-filled skies over Yellowstone, with steam from hot springs providing a dramatic foreground. The Milky Way is visible from April through

October, and the aurora borealis occasionally appears. Explore the park after dark with flashlights, friends, and bear spray for safety.

SUNRISES AND SUNSETS: The western shore of Yellowstone Lake offers breathtaking sunrise views, while the Lower Geyser Basin's hot springs and geysers are beautifully backlit at sunset. The golden hour provides the perfect light for capturing stunning images.

WILDFLOWERS AND WINTER LANDSCAPES: In July, Dunraven Pass is adorned with wildflowers, creating a colorful carpet on the slopes. Winter transforms Yellowstone into a wonderland, with snow and ice clinging to every surface, offering unique photographic opportunities of frosted trees and steaming hot springs.

SHARING AND COMMERCIAL PHOTOGRAPHY

For inspiration, visit Yellowstone's Flickr albums at: *https://www.flickr.com/photos/yellowstonenps* and follow @YellowstoneNPS on social media platforms like Facebook, Instagram, and Twitter. If you plan to profit from your images or videos, review the park's guidelines on commercial film and photography permits. By following these guidelines and respecting the park's rules, photographers can help preserve Yellowstone's natural beauty while capturing its wonders. Whether you're aiming to shoot wildlife, landscapes, or the night sky, Yellowstone promises an unforgettable experience through your lens.

RANGER-LED PROGRAMS

Participating in a ranger-led program is one of the best ways to fully experience and appreciate the natural beauty and unique features of Yellowstone National Park. These programs offer you a chance to learn more about the park's history, geology, wildlife, and ecology through the expertise of knowledgeable rangers. Here's a guide to the ranger-led programs available throughout the year at Yellowstone. | **SUMMER RANGER PROGRAMS:** During the summer season, from Memorial Day weekend through September, Yellowstone offers a wide array of ranger-led programs. These activities are designed to educate and engage visitors of all ages. The park's calendar provides specific details about the available programs, which may include guided walks, evening talks, wildlife viewing opportunities, and special events. To plan your visit and ensure you don't miss out on these enriching experiences, you can check the calendar, the Yellowstone newspaper, or the official NPS App for daily activity schedules and special pop-up programs. | **FALL RANGER PROGRAMS:** As summer transitions into fall, Yellowstone's ranger programs continue, though the schedule may be reduced. You are encouraged to check locally for the most up-to-date information on available programs. This season offers a unique opportunity to experience the park with fewer crowds and vibrant autumn colors. | **WINTER RANGER PROGRAMS:** Winter in Yellowstone transforms the park into a snowy wonderland, and ranger programs adapt to this change. Details for the 2023-2024 winter season will be available closer to the time, so visitors should check back for updates. Winter programs might include guided snowshoe walks, wildlife tracking, and educational talks about the park's winter ecology. | **SPRING RANGER PROGRAMS:** Spring is a transitional period in Yellowstone, and as such, no ranger programs are scheduled during this time. However, visitors can still explore the park on their own and enjoy the emerging signs of spring, such as blooming wildflowers and migrating wildlife. | **JUNIOR RANGER PROGRAM:** For young visitors,

Yellowstone offers a Junior Ranger program designed for children aged 4 and older. This self-guided program introduces children to the park's natural wonders and encourages them to learn about hydrothermal features, wildlife, and conservation. To participate, families can pick up a full-color Junior Ranger booklet at any visitor center or download it before arriving. Upon completing the booklet's age-appropriate activities, children can have their work reviewed by a park ranger and receive an official Yellowstone Junior Ranger badge, modeled after the National Park Service patch. | **YOUNG SCIENTIST PROGRAM:** For budding scientists, Yellowstone's Young Scientist program is available for children aged 5 and older. This program involves solving science mysteries through investigation both in visitor centers and the field. Participants can request a self-guiding booklet at the Canyon Visitor Education Center or Old Faithful Visitor Education Center. The program is tailored to different age groups, with special activities for those aged 5-9 available only at the Old Faithful Visitor Education Center. Completing the program earns young scientists an official patch (for ages 5-13) or a keychain (for ages 14+). | **VISITOR CENTERS:** Yellowstone's visitor centers are hubs of information and activity. Here, visitors can explore exhibits, participate in interpretive offerings, and speak directly with park rangers. Visitor centers provide resources for planning your visit and offer insights into the park's history, geology, and wildlife.

STAYING INFORMED

To make the most of your visit, be sure to utilize the official NPS Yellowstone App, which offers detailed information about ranger programs, self-guided tours, and other park activities. The app allows you to virtually take a ranger with you, enriching your experience with in-depth knowledge about the park's magnificent natural and cultural wonders.

Whether you're joining a guided walk, attending an evening talk, or engaging in a Junior Ranger activity, ranger-led programs at Yellowstone National Park provide invaluable opportunities to connect with the natural world and deepen your understanding of this iconic landscape.

THE OFFICIAL NPS APP

The National Park Service (NPS) App is a free, essential tool for exploring over 400 national parks in the United States. Available on iOS (*https://apps.apple.com/us/app/national-park-service/id1549226484*) and Android (*https://play.google.com/store/apps/details? id=gov.nps.mobileapp&pli=1*), it provides interactive maps to locate yourself and nearby points of interest, plan routes, and discover new areas to explore. For Yellowstone National Park, it offers real-time updates on geyser predictions, self-guided tours, and information on park amenities. The app is inclusive, with features like audio-described sites and offline content for areas with limited cell reception. Users can create virtual postcards, find activity suggestions, and stay updated with park news and alerts. The NPS App is designed to enhance and enrich your national park experience with its comprehensive features and user-friendly interface.

HISTORIC SITES AND MUSEUMS

While Yellowstone National Park is primarily known for its natural wonders, there are also a few historic sites and museums within the park that offer insights into its cultural and historical significance. Here are some notable places to explore:

GRAND LOOP ROAD HISTORIC DISTRICT

The Grand Loop Road Historic District encompasses the main road that forms a loop through Yellowstone National Park. This district includes various historic features, such as bridges, overlooks, and other structures along the road. These structures showcase the park's architectural heritage and provide scenic viewpoints for visitors to enjoy.

FISHING BRIDGE HISTORIC DISTRICT

Situated near Yellowstone Lake, the Fishing Bridge Historic District includes the historic Fishing Bridge. Once a popular spot for angling, the bridge now serves as a pedestrian walkway. It offers visitors an opportunity to appreciate the area's natural beauty and observe the lake's wildlife.

LAKE FISH HATCHERY HISTORIC DISTRICT

Located near Yellowstone Lake, the Lake Fish Hatchery Historic District houses a historic fish hatchery that was instrumental in fish conservation and stocking efforts. Visitors can learn about the park's fishery management practices and witness the hatchery's operations.

LAMAR BUFFALO RANCH DISTRICT

The Lamar Buffalo Ranch District encompasses the historic buffalo ranch, which played a significant role in bison conservation efforts. Situated in the picturesque Lamar Valley, the district offers visitors a glimpse into the park's conservation history and the ongoing efforts to protect and preserve its wildlife.

MAMMOTH HOT SPRINGS HISTORIC DISTRICT

Located near the park's North Entrance, the Mammoth Hot Springs

Historic District is home to the stunning Mammoth Hot Springs Terraces. These unique limestone formations and travertine terraces are a result of the area's geothermal activity. Additionally, the district includes historic structures such as Fort Yellowstone, which served as the park's administrative headquarters, and the Mammoth Post Office.

NORTH ENTRANCE ROAD HISTORIC DISTRICT

The North Entrance Road Historic District comprises the historic road leading to the North Entrance of Yellowstone National Park. This scenic road offers visitors access to the park and showcases the natural beauty of the surrounding landscape.

OLD FAITHFUL AREA HISTORIC DISTRICT

The Old Faithful Area Historic District is a focal point of Yellowstone National Park. It encompasses the iconic Old Faithful Inn, a grand log hotel known for its unique architecture and rustic charm. Visitors can explore the inn, admire its craftsmanship, and enjoy the nearby geothermal features. The district also includes the Queen's Laundry Bathhouse, adding to its historical significance.

ROOSEVELT LODGE HISTORIC DISTRICT

The Roosevelt Lodge Historic District is located in the Tower-Roosevelt area of the park. The district is centered around the historic Roosevelt Lodge, which offers rustic accommodations and a glimpse into the park's early days. Visitors can experience the lodge's historic charm and explore the surrounding natural beauty.

OBSIDIAN CLIFF KIOSK

Obsidian Cliff kiosk, Yellowstone National Park, Wyoming, USA - Photo by Wikimedia user Acroterion

The Obsidian Cliff Kiosk, built in 1931, is a historic structure in Yellowstone National Park near Obsidian Cliff. It serves as an interpretive site, providing information on the geological and cultural significance of the area. The kiosk explains the history of the Obsidian Cliff, known for its high-quality volcanic glass, which Native Americans extensively mined for tools and weapons. The displays detail obsidian formation, ancient quarrying methods, and trade networks distributing obsidian artifacts across North America. Part of the Mammoth Hot Springs Historic District, the kiosk underscores the National Park Service's dedication to conservation and public education.

QUEEN'S LAUNDRY BATHHOUSE

The Queen's Laundry Bathhouse is a historic bathhouse located in the Old Faithful Area Historic District. It served as a facility for visitors to wash and bathe during their stay in the park. Today, it stands as a reminder of the park's early infrastructure & accommodations.

MAMMOTH POST OFFICE

The Mammoth Post Office, built in 1939, is a historic building within the Mammoth Hot Springs Historic District in Yellowstone National Park, Wyoming. It exemplifies the rustic architectural style of the early 20th century National Park Service, using native materials like local stone and timber to blend with its natural surroundings. Serving both park employees and visitors, it offers various postal services, highlighting the importance of such facilities in remote areas. The post office is also a significant example of historic preservation, retaining its original features and representing the New Deal era's impact on enhancing national park infrastructure.

Yellowstone National Park - Mammoth Hot Springs - US Post Office
- Photo By Wikipedia User JrozwadoRoosevelt Arch

Roosevelt Arch in Gardiner, Montana, at the entrance to Yellowstone National Park - photo by Wikimedia user Acroterion

The Roosevelt Arch, located at the North Entrance of Yellowstone National Park near Gardiner, Montana, is a historic structure dedicated by President Theodore Roosevelt on April 24, 1903. Constructed of local basalt stone and standing 50 feet tall, the arch features a central archway and two smaller passageways. It bears the inscription "For the Benefit and Enjoyment of the People," reflecting the mission of the National Park Service to preserve natural wonders for public enjoyment. The arch symbolizes the early conservation efforts and the significance of Yellowstone as the first national park. It remains a popular landmark, representing the values of preservation and public access.

THE QUEEN'S LAUNDRY BATHHOUSE

The Queen's Laundry Bathhouse in Yellowstone National Park's Old Faithful Area is a historic building from the early 1900s. It once served as a facility for visitors to wash and bathe during their stay in the park. While it is no longer in operation, the bathhouse reflects the rustic architectural style of the park, featuring log construction and a functional design. Today, it stands as a reminder of the park's early accommodations and visitor services, allowing visitors to appreciate its historical significance and imagine life for early Yellowstone guests

FISHING BRIDGE MUSEUM

Located near the Fishing Bridge, this museum highlights the history and ecology of Yellowstone Lake. Exhibits focus on the lake's fish species, early angling history, and the challenges of managing the lake's ecosystem.

MADISON MUSEUM

These small museums are situated along the respective trails within Yellowstone National Park. They provide informative exhibits and displays about the park's natural and cultural history. Visitors can learn about the geology, flora, fauna, and human impact on the park's ecosystem.

NORRIS MUSEUM

The Norris Museum, located near the Norris Geyser Basin in Yellowstone National Park, was built in 1929 and showcases the park's unique geothermal features and geology. The museum's rustic architectural style is typical of National Park Service buildings from that era. Strategically positioned in a highly active geothermal area, the museum offers exhibits on geysers, hot springs, fumaroles, and mud pots, along with interactive displays illustrating the underlying geothermal processes and geological history. It highlights the Norris Geyser Basin's dynamic nature, featuring geysers like Steamboat Geyser, the world's tallest active geyser. The museum emphasizes the importance of preserving these natural wonders and the National Park Service's role in their protection, making it an essential destination for those interested in natural sciences and Yellowstone's geothermal phenomena.

Norris, Madison, and Fishing Bridge Museums

FORT YELLOWSTONE

Fort Yellowstone is a historic site that includes various buildings and structures that once served as the administrative headquarters of Yellowstone National Park during its early years. These structures are located in the Mammoth Hot Springs Historic District, and they played a crucial role in managing the park, enforcing regulations, and protecting its resources.

Norris Geyser Basin Museum

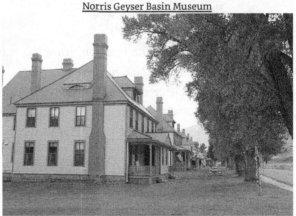

Officer Housing, Fort Yellowstone, Yellowstone National
Park - Photo from Wikimedia user Acroterion

NORTHEAST ENTRANCE STATION

The Northeast Entrance Station is a historic structure located at the park's northeast entrance. It represents an important entry point to Yellowstone National Park and offers visitors a sense of arrival and transition into the park's unique natural environment.

Northeast Entrance Station

OBSIDIAN CLIFF ARCHEOLOGICAL SITE

The Obsidian Cliff Archeological Site is a significant location within the park, known for its ancient Native American quarries. These quarries provided a vital source of obsidian, a volcanic glass used by indigenous peoples for making tools and weapons. The site offers visitors an opportunity to learn about the region's cultural history and archaeological significance.

OLD FAITHFUL INN

The Old Faithful Inn is a grand and iconic log hotel located in the Old Faithful Area Historic District. Built in 1903-1904, it showcases a unique blend of rustic architecture and craftsmanship. Visitors can explore the inn's historic interior, admire the massive log structure, and experience the charm of its common areas and guest rooms.

Old Faithful Inn, Yellowstone National Park - Photo by Wikimedia User Grahampurse

LAKE HOTEL

The Lake Hotel is a historic hotel situated near Yellowstone Lake. Built in 1891, it stands as one of the oldest and most elegant lodging options in the park. The hotel offers guests a glimpse into the park's past, combined with modern amenities and stunning lake views.

Yellowstone Lake Hotel, Yellowstone National Park

YELLOWSTONE HISTORIC CENTER
IN WEST YELLOWSTONE

This center, located just outside the west entrance of Yellowstone National Park, showcases exhibits and artifacts related to the park's history, including its early exploration, the establishment of the park, Native American history, and the development of tourism. You can learn about the volcanic activity, hydrothermal processes, and the unique ecosystem that exists in Yellowstone.

Yellowstone Historic Center in West Yellowstone

These historic districts, buildings, and sites contribute to the rich cultural and historical heritage of Yellowstone National Park, allowing visitors to appreciate the park's natural wonders alongside its significant past. While Yellowstone's historic sites and museums may not be as numerous as its natural attractions, they provide an opportunity to delve into the park's cultural and historical aspects, adding depth to your visit.

Grand Teton National Park - Near Jackson Lake Lodge BY chascar

CHAPTER 4: WHAT TO SEE & DO AT THE GRAND TETON NATIONAL PARK

- Grand Teton Range and Scenic Drives
- Jenny Lake and Hiking Trails
- Wildlife and Bird Watching
- Outdoor Adventures
- Climbing and Mountaineering
- Rafting and Kayaking
- Visitor Centers and Interpretive Programs

TOP 10 MUST-SEE FEATURES OF
GRAND TETON NATIONAL PARK

The Grand Teton National Park is renowned for its stunning mountain range, pristine lakes, and abundant wildlife. Here are some of the top 10 attractions and activities to experience in the park:

- Grand Teton Range
- Jenny Lake
- Signal Mountain
- Snake River
- Mormon Row Historic District
- Taggart Lake
- Schwabacher Landing
- Chapel of the Transfiguration
- Laurance S. Rockefeller Preserve
- Colter Bay Village

1. THE TETON RANGE

The majestic Teton Range is the centerpiece of the park, offering breathtaking views and ample opportunities for hiking, photography, and scenic drives. The dramatic peaks, including Grand Teton, Middle Teton, and South Teton, provide a stunning backdrop for outdoor adventures. Gazing upon the Tetons for the first time is an unforgettable experience. The mountain range is awe-inspiring in its magnitude and drama. There are countless ways to experience the Tetons, all of them equally extraordinary. Adventures of all sizes await in this majestic range, whether you visit in winter or summer. Here are the top activities to make the most of your time in the Teton Range.

WINTER ACTIVITIES

SKIING: The Tetons are renowned for their steep slopes and deep snow. Jackson Hole Mountain Resort offers direct access to these thrilling terrains. For a different perspective, Grand Targhee in Alta provides stunning views from the other side of the range. For a more rugged experience, consider backcountry skiing with a local guide, recommended for strong skiers with avalanche safety knowledge.

NORDIC SKIING: Cross-country skiing offers an intimate way to experience the Tetons' winter scenery. Tour through quiet forests to Taggart Lake or enjoy the groomed park road in Grand Teton National Park, which accommodates cross-country skiing, skate skiing, and snowshoeing.

FAT BIKING: Fat bikes, equipped with extra-wide tires, make cycling a year-round activity. In Grand Teton National Park, fat bikes are allowed on roadways open to cars, providing a unique, low-impact way to explore the snowy landscape.

SUMMER ACTIVITIES

HIKING: With hundreds of miles of trails, the Tetons are a hiker's paradise. Start your adventure at String or Jenny Lake and choose from numerous trails. For a longer trek, take the Jenny Lake ferry and hike into Cascade Canyon for a 10-mile journey with stunning views. For a mellower day, visit Hidden Falls or Inspiration Point, or explore the trails around the lake.

FLOATING: A float trip down the Snake River in Grand Teton National Park is one of the best ways to see wildlife and appreciate the serene beauty of the Tetons. The slow-moving, braided river offers opportunities to spot waterfowl, eagles, beavers, river otters, and large mammals like moose. A river guide is recommended for navigating the technical waters.

HORSEBACK RIDING: Feel like a true Wyomingite by tackling Teton trails on horseback. Numerous outfitters in the Jackson area offer horseback riding tours for all experience levels. Enjoy the meditative rhythm of your horse's gait as you traverse alpine meadows, creeks, and forests while keeping an eye out for wildlife.

CLIMBING: The Tetons are a dream destination for climbers. With experienced outfitters like Exum Mountain Guides, climbing the Grand Teton is entirely possible. For those seeking less committal climbs, mountain guides can introduce you to the ropes and the rugged rock faces of the Tetons.

2. JENNY LAKE

Jenny Lake is a must-visit destination in Grand Teton National Park, offering a variety of activities that cater to all interests and abilities. Named after the Shoshone wife of a trapper, Jenny Lake's picturesque shores and pristine waters make it a hub for hikers, boaters, campers, and nature lovers. This iconic glacial lake offers crystal-clear waters nestled among towering peaks. You can hike the picturesque Jenny Lake Loop Trail, take a boat ride across the lake, or embark on more challenging hikes to destinations like Hidden Falls and Inspiration Point. | **THE BASICS:** Situated at the base of Cascade Canyon, Jenny Lake spans nearly two square miles of crystal-clear mountain water. It's one of only two lakes in Jackson Hole where motorboat access is allowed, and it offers a scenic shuttle service across its waters, unlike the larger Jackson Lake to the north. The area features the charming Jenny Lake Lodge, where you can enjoy fine dining with a reservation. | **LAYOUT:** Jenny Lake is divided into two main areas: South Jenny Lake and North Jenny Lake. The South area is more developed, with amenities such as a visitor center, ranger station, campground, and docks. North Jenny Lake is quieter, featuring a boat launch, picnic area, and trailhead. | **GETTING THERE:** Jenny Lake is easily accessible from Teton Park Road, with multiple signs indicating the North and South recreation areas. Park passes are required and cost $35 per car for a seven-day pass. Arrive early in the morning or late in the afternoon to avoid the crowds and limited parking. | **SOUTH JENNY LAKE:** Begin your adventure at the Jenny Lake Visitor Center, which offers informational displays and interactive presentations about the area's natural history and geology. The visitor center is open daily from June 1 to September 4. From here, you can obtain backcountry permits, stock up on provisions at the general store, or book trips with Exum Mountain Guides. | **HIKING:** Jenny Lake is a hiker's paradise with trails suitable for all levels. Popular routes include: _Jenny Lake Trail:_ A 7.1-mile loop around the lake. | _String Lake Trail:_ A 3.7-mile loop around String Lake. | _Leigh Lake Trail:_ An out-and-back hike along the eastern shore of Leigh Lake. | _Hidden Falls and Inspiration Point:_ Accessible from the Jenny Lake shoreline, these destinations offer stunning views and are perfect for a shorter hike. | **CAMPING:** The Jenny Lake campground is one of the park's most popular spots for overnight stays. Campgrounds cost $30 per night per site, or $15 for seniors and cardholders. Reservations must be made and paid for six months in advance. | **BOATING:** Whether you rent a canoe or kayak from the South Jenny Lake docks, launch your own motorized vessel (with an engine under 10 horsepower), or take the Jenny Lake ferry, the lake's glassy waters are perfect for an afternoon voyage. Kayak and canoe rentals cost $20 per hour or $80 per day. Motor boating permits are available at the visitor center for $20 per day or $40 annually. The Jenny Lake shuttle, departing every 15 minutes from South Jenny Lake, provides a scenic and practical way to reach the Cascade Canyon trailhead. Round trips cost $18 for adults, $15 for seniors, and $10 for children. One-way tickets are also available. | **CYCLING:** Jenny Lake's multi-use pathways offer extensive bike-friendly terrain. Ride your bike from the town of Jackson or choose from two loops within the park: an 8-mile route from Moose to South Jenny Lake or a 4-mile trip from the Taggart Lake trailhead to Jenny Lake. Biking is a great way to bypass parking issues and enjoy the scenic views. | **SCENIC DRIVE:** For a breathtaking photo opportunity, follow the signs at North Jenny Lake Junction to reach the Cascade Canyon Overlook. This narrow, one-way road will take you to the South Jenny Lake Junction, offering stunning views along the way. Drive slowly and watch for pedestrians, bikers, and wildlife.

3. SIGNAL MOUNTAIN

Signal Mountain is a central and convenient basecamp for those exploring Grand Teton National Park (GTNP). Nestled adjacent to the Signal Mountain Lodge on the southeast shore of Jackson Lake, this 80-site campground provides easy access to the lake and short walks to breathtaking views of the Teton Range. The area teems with wildlife, making it a prime spot for nature enthusiasts and bird watchers.

SIGNAL MOUNTAIN CAMPGROUND: Signal Mountain Campground is one of the first campgrounds to open and the last to close in the park, often with lingering snowpack during opening weeks and early winter weather at the season's end. Visitors should prepare for variable weather, especially in May and October.

SIGNAL MOUNTAIN LODGE & MARINA: Located in the heart of Grand Teton National Park, Signal Mountain Lodge & Marina is the only lakefront accommodation in the park. It offers a range of lodging options, from cozy one-room mountain cabins to suite-style units with kitchenettes, all with stunning views of the Grand Tetons. The lodge also features a marina, dining experiences with western favorites, and guided fishing tours.

HIKING THE SIGNAL MOUNTAIN TRAIL: The hike to Signal Mountain begins from the Signal Mountain Lodge parking area. The trail offers a moderate challenge with a 6.8-mile roundtrip length, a total elevation gain of 920 feet, and an average elevation gain of 271 feet per mile. The highest elevation point is at 7,593 feet. | **Trailhead Location:** Signal Mountain Lodge, 3 miles south of Jackson Lake Junction and 17.6 miles north of Moose Junction. | ***Directions:*** From Jackson, WY, take Route 89 north towards Moran. Enter Grand Teton National Park, take a left on the main park road, pass over the Snake River, and continue for a few miles before turning left onto Signal Mountain Road. It's about 5 miles to the top from this road. | ***Trail Highlights:*** The Signal Mountain Trail offers panoramic views, wildlife sightings, and a taste of history. Although the trail doesn't reach the 7,720-foot summit, it provides outstanding vistas of the Grand Tetons, Jackson Lake, and the Snake River from the Jackson Point Overlook. | ***Trail Description:*** Starting from the parking area, hikers cross Teton Park Road and make a steep climb to Signal

Mountain Road. Shortly after crossing the road, the trail passes a pleasant lily pond, where moose sightings are common. Hikers will have excellent views of Mt. Moran at roughly two-thirds of a mile. | **Trail Loop:** At seven-tenths of a mile, a fork marks the beginning of a short loop. Taking the right fork (Lake Trail) offers great views of the Grand Tetons on the way up, while the left fork (Ridge Trail) provides scenic vistas during the descent. | ***Wildlife and Scenery:*** The southern loop passes a small lake frequented by moose, black bears, mule deer, ducks, and other waterfowl. The northern loop offers a more open terrain with sweeping views of the Grand Tetons and wildflower displays in early-to-mid summer. | ***Jackson Point Overlook:*** At 3.5 miles, hikers reach Jackson Point Overlook, a perch offering stunning views of the Grand Tetons, Jackson Lake, Jackson Hole, and the Gros Ventre Mountains. This overlook is named after William Henry Jackson, who captured the first photographs of the Grand Tetons and Jackson Hole during the 1871 and 1878 Hayden Geological Surveys. | **HISTORICAL SIGNIFICANCE:** Signal Mountain received its name after a suspicious incident in 1890. John Dudley Sargent and Robert Ray Hamilton, a great-grandson of Alexander Hamilton, ran the nearby Merymere Lodge. During a hunting trip, Hamilton went missing, and search parties were instructed to light a "signal" fire atop the mountain upon finding him. A week later, his body was found floating in the Snake River, leading to speculation about foul play involving Sargent.

4. THE SNAKE RIVER

The Snake River, a defining feature of Grand Teton National Park, winds its way through the valley floor, carrying snowmelt from the towering Teton Range westward toward the Pacific Ocean. This river, essential to the park's ecosystem, offers breathtaking views of the Tetons and is a vital resource for wildlife, including moose and beaver. Floating down the Snake River provides an unforgettable way to experience the park's natural beauty and wildlife.

EXPLORING THE SNAKE RIVER

The Snake River's journey is intricate, with numerous channels that shift yearly. Navigating this powerful river requires skill in river reading and navigation. Before embarking on a float, it's crucial to understand the skills needed, know the route, and have the necessary equipment. The river's complexity is evident in its various sections, each offering different levels of challenge:

BEGINNER SECTION: *Jackson Lake Dam to Pacific Creek (5 miles):* This stretch features scenic views, calmer waters, and few obstructions. Boaters should scout the swift water at Pacific Creek landing before launching.

INTERMEDIATE SECTIONS: *Pacific Creek to Deadmans Bar (10 miles):* This section has significant drops, creating swift water and braided channels that require careful route-finding. | *Flagg Ranch to Lizard Creek Campground (10 miles):* The braided channels in this stretch make navigation challenging. Depending on Jackson Lake's level, strenuous rowing or paddling may be required, especially if afternoon thunderstorms produce waves.

ADVANCED SECTIONS: *Deadmans Bar to Moose Landing (10 miles):* Known for its steep drops and complex braiding, this is the park's most challenging section. Strong currents can sweep boaters into side channels blocked by logjams. | *Moose to Wilson (14 miles):* This stretch is equally difficult, requiring advanced boating skills due to fast currents, braided channels, and logjams. | *Flagg Canyon (Southgate to Flagg Ranch, 3 miles):* South of Yellowstone National Park, this section features challenging white water with Class III rapids during heavy spring flows. Canoeing in these conditions requires advanced white water skills.

RIVER ETIQUETTE AND SAFETY: To ensure a safe and enjoyable experience on the Snake River, it's important to follow river etiquette: Prepare boats away from launch ramps to reduce congestion. | Launch when other boats are out of sight and maintain this interval throughout your trip. | Avoid playing loud music to respect other boaters and wildlife. | Steer clear of other boaters and anglers.

| Checking flow rates before each trip is essential, as they vary throughout the year. Spring flows are cold, fast, and muddy, making the river more difficult, while summer flows are slower but still powerful. Essential equipment includes a personal flotation device (PFD), proper footwear, layers, a knife, drinking water and snacks, a whistle, a first aid kit, and a throw bag.

SCENIC FLOATING AND DRIFT BOATING: Floating down the Snake River is a serene way to experience the grandeur of the Tetons and the local wildlife. Whether using an old-school inner-tube, a wooden drift boat, or a heavy-duty raft, a leisurely float offers a unique perspective of the park's beauty. Outfitters in Jackson Hole provide guided services and rentals for canoes, kayaks, rafts, and "duckies."

Drift boating, a traditional mode of river navigation in Jackson, offers a classic experience. These wooden or fiberglass boats, steered by oars, can navigate shallow channels and tricky eddies. Local outfitter AJ DeRosa's company, Jackson Hole Vintage Adventures, uses hand-made drift boats crafted by the guides themselves, adding an artisan twist to the river adventure.

HIGH-ADRENALINE ADVENTURES: For those seeking more excitement, the Snake River Canyon offers an eight-mile stretch of whitewater with Class II and III rapids. This area is popular with kayakers looking for a challenge. Stand-up paddleboarding (SUPping) is another popular activity, allowing enthusiasts to surf the river on extra-wide surfboards.

FLY FISHING ON THE SNAKE RIVER: Jackson Hole is a renowned destination for fly fishing, particularly for the fine-spotted cutthroat trout unique to the Snake River watershed. Fishing from a drift boat, wading through creeks, or casting from the riverbank offers unique challenges and rewards throughout the year. Catch-and-release fishing is permitted year-round, and a fishing license is required.

GUIDED RAFT TRIPS: A guided Wild & Scenic Raft Trip down the Snake River is a must-do activity, offering scenic 10-mile floats with expert guides sharing knowledge about local flora, fauna, and history. These trips provide close-up views of wildlife, including bald eagles, moose, bison, elk, osprey, and beavers, with picnic-style lunch options available.

The Snake River offers a diverse range of activities for visitors of all skill levels, from tranquil scenic floats to thrilling whitewater adventures, making it a quintessential part of the park's experience.

5. MORMON ROW HISTORIC DISTRICT

Mormon Row, originally known as the town of Grovont, is a historical district within Grand Teton National Park that was settled in the late 1890s by Mormons from the Salt Lake region. This community was established under the Homestead Act of 1862, which granted land ownership to individuals willing to build a house and cultivate the land for five years. Settlers in Mormon Row secured 27 homesteads, building their homes close together to facilitate the sharing of labor and fostering a strong sense of community. | **AGRICULTURAL CHALLENGES AND INNOVATIONS:** Settlers of Mormon Row faced significant challenges, including the need to irrigate their fields. They dug extensive ditches to transport water from the Gros Ventre River. During winter, these ditches would freeze, forcing families to gather water directly from the river. A dependable water source wasn't available until 1927, when the Kelly Warm Spring cooled due to hydrologic shifts from the Gros Ventre slide flood. This allowed for year-round water access. The primary crops were hay and ninety-day oats, chosen for their ability to endure Jackson Hole's short growing season and harsh conditions. In addition to crops, families raised cows for milk and meat, and horses for tilling the fields. | **COMMUNITY AND HISTORICAL STRUCTURES:** At its peak, Grovont was home to multiple ranches, homes, a church, and a school. The church, built in 1916, served as a social hub for the entire community, regardless of faith. Although the building was moved to Wilson, its original location is marked by fence posts, two cottonwoods, and a spruce tree. In the mid-1900s, Mormon Row was acquired to expand Grand Teton National Park. By

1997, it was added to the National Register of Historic Places. Today, several barns from the original homesteads still stand, offering a glimpse into the area's history.

ICONIC BARNS OF MORMON ROW

JOHN MOULTON BARN: _History:_ Part of John and Bartha Moulton's homestead, this barn, along with their pink stucco home, is one of the most photographed structures in the area. | _Significance:_ The homestead was inhabited seasonally until the late 1980s. | **T.A. MOULTON BARN:** _History:_ Located just south of his brother John's homestead, T.A. Moulton's barn took over 30 years to build. | _Significance:_ This barn, along with the John Moulton barn, is a popular subject for photographers due to its picturesque backdrop of the Teton Range. | **CHAMBERS BARN:** _History:_ Built by Andrew (Andy) and Ida Chambers, this barn is part of the most intact homestead remaining at Mormon Row. | _Significance:_ Andy Chambers secured his homestead title by building a log cabin and stable, and clearing land for crops. He also built a windmill for electricity, which still stands. The homestead was added to the National Register of Historic Places in 1990 and to the Mormon Row district in 1997. | **THOMAS MURPHY BARN/REED MOULTON BARN:** _History:_ Initially built by Thomas Murphy and later owned by Joe Heninger, who held the mail contract for the Jackson to Moran route. | _Significance:_ Heninger provided his homestead as a rest stop for mail drivers and their horses during winter. | **CLARK & VEDA MOULTON HOMESTEAD:** _History:_ Clark Moulton, T.A. Moulton's son, received a one-acre plot from his father upon marrying Veda in 1936. | _Significance:_ The house they built on this plot remains standing and is the last privately owned property on Mormon Row. | Exploring Mormon Row offers visitors a unique window into the past, showcasing the resilience and ingenuity of early settlers in the region. The preserved structures and surrounding landscape provide a tangible connection to the history and heritage of the area.t

6. TAGGART LAKE

Located near the park's southern entrance, Taggart and Bradley Lakes offer picturesque settings for leisurely hikes and scenic picnics. The trail to the lakes showcases breathtaking views of the Teton Range and takes visitors through serene forests. Wildlife sightings, including moose and beavers, are also possible in this area. These tranquil lakes provide a serene escape and a chance to immerse yourself in the natural beauty of the park.

HIKING TAGGART LAKE TRAIL

Taggart Lake is an easy, out-and-back trail located in Grand Teton National Park, offering some of the best views of the Teton Range. The trail starts from the Taggart Lake Trailhead and winds through aspen-covered moraines, providing hikers with spectacular views of the Tetons.

TRAIL DETAILS: *Distance:* 3 miles roundtrip | *Duration:* 1-2 hours | *Elevation Gain:* 360 feet | *Trail Type:* Out-and-back | *Difficulty:* Easy | *Pets:* Not allowed | *Fees:* Entrance fees required for the national park | *Restrooms:* Available at the trailhead | *Season*: Year-round | *Accessibility:* Trail includes rocks and steps with a 6% average slope.

DIRECTIONS AND PARKING: *Trailhead Location:* Access the trailhead from the Teton Park Road, three and a half miles northwest from Moose Junction. | *Parking:* Limited parking at the trailhead; arrive early to secure a spot.

HIKING EXPERIENCE: *Trail Start:* Begins at the large parking lot at the Taggart Lake Trailhead. | *Initial Split:* About 0.13 miles in, the trail splits; take the right fork to continue towards Taggart Lake. | *Creek Crossing:* Shortly after the split, cross a small creek and pass through historic farmland. | *Aspen and Pine Forests:* Continue through dense aspen and pine forests with changing foliage in the fall. | *Mountain Views:* The trail opens up to stunning views of the Teton Range before reaching the lake. | *Final Approach:* A final forested section leads to the lakeshore, offering beautiful views of the alpine lake with the Tetons as a backdrop.

POINTS OF INTEREST: *Historic Farmland:* Old structures and houses can be seen near the trail. | *Aspen and Pine Forests:* Dense forests provide shade and beautiful scenery. | *Mountain Views:* Clearings offer panoramic views of the Tetons. | *Taggart Lake:* Crystal clear water reflecting the Teton Range; great for photos and relaxation.

ADDITIONAL LOOP OPTION: *Taggart Lake-Beaver Creek Loop:* A 3.9-mile loop that includes Beaver Creek, offering an extended hike with additional scenic views and moderate elevation gain (500 feet).

WILDLIFE AND SAFETY: **Wildlife:** Possible sightings of moose, deer, and bears; travel in groups, make noise, and carry bear spray. | **Safety Tips:** Bring plenty of water (at least 2 liters), wear appropriate footwear, and start early to avoid crowds and high temperatures.

BEST TIME TO HIKE: *Summer and Fall:* Ideal seasons with pleasant weather and vibrant fall colors. | *Early Morning or Evening:* To avoid crowds and enjoy cooler temperatures.

Taggart Lake is a highly recommended hike for its easy trail, stunning views, and beautiful lake setting. Despite its popularity, it's a rewarding hike with plenty of opportunities for photography and wildlife observation.

7. SCHWABACHER LANDING

Schwabacher Landing is a stunning location that epitomizes the grandeur of Grand Teton National Park. Situated 16 miles north of Jackson, Wyoming, this picturesque spot offers unparalleled views of the Teton Mountains, mirrored perfectly in the still waters of the Snake River. The area's serene beauty makes it a prime destination for photographers, nature enthusiasts, and outdoor adventurers. Schwabacher Landing is one of the most picturesque spots in Grand Teton National Park, known for its stunning reflections of the Teton Range in the still waters of the Snake River. This area is a favorite among photographers, especially during sunrise and sunset, when the alpenglow lights up the peaks. It also offers opportunities for wildlife viewing, including moose, beavers, and various bird species. Visitors can enjoy the serene beauty of the landscape from several viewpoints along the river.

LOCATION AND ACCESS: Getting to Schwabacher Landing is straightforward. From Jackson Hole, travel north on Highway 89 for about 16 miles. Look for a small gravel road on the left, marked by a wooden sign reading "Schwabacher's Landing Road." This road leads to a gravel parking lot, from where a short walk will take you to the famous vantage point.

BEST TIME TO VISIT: Summer and fall are the ideal seasons to visit Schwabacher Landing. During these times, the gravel road is most accessible, and the weather is generally favorable for outdoor activities. The road can become impassable in inclement weather during other seasons, so plan your visit accordingly.

ACTIVITIES: Schwabacher Landing offers a variety of activities for visitors: **Photography:** The reflection of the Teton Mountains in the calm Snake River creates a majestic scene, making Schwabacher Landing a top spot for photography. | **Wildlife Watching:** The area is rich in wildlife. Visitors can expect to see coyote, antelope, deer, otter, and eagles among other animals. | **Hiking:** A four-mile hiking trail winds along the banks of the Snake River, passing by beaver dams and offering continuous views of the Tetons and their reflections. | **Fishing and River Rafting:** The flat terrain and easy river access make Schwabacher Landing a popular launch site for anglers and river rafters. Guided float trips and duckie tours are available through local providers, such as National Park Float Trips and Rendezvous River Sports. | **Family-Friendly Excursion:** Schwabacher Landing is an excellent spot for a family outing. The flat terrain and scenic views provide a perfect setting for a day of exploring. Pack a picnic and enjoy a leisurely day surrounded by nature's splendor. The abundant wildlife and beautiful landscapes ensure a memorable experience for visitors of all ages.

A visit to Schwabacher Landing in Grand Teton National Park offers a unique blend of natural beauty, wildlife viewing, and outdoor recreation. Whether you're a seasoned photographer, a wildlife enthusiast, or simply looking for a peaceful spot to enjoy nature, Schwabacher Landing is a must-visit destination.

8. CHAPEL OF THE TRANSFIGURATION

The Chapel of the Transfiguration is a quaint log chapel located in Grand Teton National Park, near Moose, Wyoming. Built in 1925 on land donated by Maud Noble, the chapel was initially constructed to provide settlers with a local place of worship, eliminating the need to travel to Jackson for church services. Today, it continues to function as an Episcopal church, offering religious services and serving as a cherished landmark within the park. The Chapel of the Transfiguration is a historic chapel located within Grand Teton National Park near Moose, Wyoming. Built in 1925, this rustic log structure features a large window behind the altar that frames a stunning view of the Teton Range. The chapel is a popular spot for weddings and visitors seeking a moment of reflection amid the natural beauty of the park. It is part of the St. John's Episcopal Church and remains an active place of worship.

LOCATION AND ACCESS: The chapel is situated just within the southern entrance of Grand Teton National Park, about 15 miles from the town of Jackson. To reach the chapel, enter the park at Moose Junction, then turn onto Chapel of the Transfiguration Road, located 1.1 miles north of Moose Junction. Follow the signs for the chapel and Menors Ferry Historic District.

VISITING INFORMATION: *Duration:* 5-60 minutes | *Activity:* Self-guided walking tours | *Pets Allowed:* No | *Activity Fee:* No | *Location:* Moose | *Reservations:* Not required | *Season:* Spring, Summer, Fall | *Time of Day:* Day, dawn, dusk | *Accessibility:* Parking available with paved, level paths

CHAPEL SERVICES AND ACTIVITIES: The Chapel of the Transfiguration continues to offer Holy Communion services every Sunday during the summer season, from late May through early September. Services are held at 8:00 a.m. and 10:00 a.m., conducted by visiting chaplains and organists from various locations.

VISITING CHAPLAINS FOR THE SUMMER: *June:* The Rev. Kirkland "Skully" Knight, Episcopal School of Baton Rouge, LA | *July:* The Rev. Lester V. Mackenzie, Rector, St. Mary's Episcopal Church, Laguna Beach, CA | *August:* The Rev. Chip Edens, Rector, Christ Church, Charlotte, NC

HIGHLIGHTS AND ACTIVITIES: *Sightseeing:* The chapel is a favorite spot for photographers and sightseers due to its rustic charm and the breathtaking view of the Teton Mountain Range framed by a large window behind the altar. | *Weddings:* The chapel's stunning backdrop makes it a popular venue for weddings. Couples can exchange vows with the majestic Tetons in the background. Arrangements for weddings can be made through St. John's Episcopal Church in Jackson.

ADDITIONAL INFORMATION: The Chapel of the Transfiguration is part of the Menors Ferry Historic District, and visitors are encouraged to be respectful as it remains an active house of worship. The chapel played a role in the 1963 movie "Spencer's Mountain," starring Henry Fonda and Maureen O'Hara.

CONTACT INFORMATION FOR WEDDINGS AND SERVICES: Chapel of the Transfiguration , c/o St. John's Episcopal Church , P.O. Box 1690 Jackson, WY 83001 | **Phone:** (307) 733-2603 | **Website:** *http://stjohnsjackson.org* | **TIPS:** No additional permits are required by the Park Service for chapel use, but admission fees to the park apply. The church may charge additional fees for private use of the chapel.

Whether visiting for a service, a wedding, or simply to take in the stunning views, the Chapel of the Transfiguration offers a serene and spiritually enriching experience amidst the natural beauty of Grand Teton National Park.

9. LAURANCE S. ROCKEFELLER PRESERVE

The Laurance S. Rockefeller Preserve Center in Grand Teton National Park offers visitors a unique experience focused on conservation and the natural beauty of the area. Dedicated to Laurance S. Rockefeller's vision of preserving and stewarding the environment, the center features engaging exhibits that stimulate the senses through various media, including a soundscape room, audio recordings, and nature photography. You can also enjoy ranger-led programs, relax in the resource room, or embark on scenic hikes to Phelps Lake.

LOCATION AND ACCESSIBILITY: *GPS Coordinates:* *Latitude:* 43° 37' 35.0976" N | *Longitude:* 110° 46' 30.8208" W | **Driving Directions:** *From Teton Village:* Head north on WY 390 for 3.2 miles past the Granite Entrance Gate and turn right (east) at the Preserve Center sign. | *From Moose:* Drive south on Teton Park Road, turn south at the sign for "Wilson Road/Teton Village 9 miles," continue 3.7 miles, and turn left (east) at the Preserve Center sign. | **NOTE:** The Preserve Center is not accessible to vehicles over 23.3 feet long or trailers due to Moose-Wilson Road construction. Parking is limited and fills up quickly, often by 9 a.m. Consider carpooling to reduce congestion.

VISITING INFORMATION: *Season:* Spring, Summer, Fall | *Time of Day:* Day, dawn, dusk | *Pets Allowed:* No | *Reservations Required:* No | *Activity Fee:* None | *Duration:* 5-60 minutes | *Accessibility:* Parking available with paved, level paths.

ACTIVITIES AND HIGHLIGHTS: *Exhibits and Programs:* Learn about Laurance S. Rockefeller's conservation legacy through sensory exhibits, including a soundscape room and nature photography. Attend ranger-led programs to deepen your understanding of the natural environment. | *Hiking:* Several trails start from the Preserve, ranging from easy hikes to Phelps Lake to more strenuous treks into Granite Canyon or Death Canyon. These trails offer opportunities to explore diverse landscapes and enjoy stunning views | *Wildlife Viewing:* The Preserve and surrounding areas are home to black bears, grizzly bears, moose, and deer. Exercise caution and maintain safe distances from wildlife | *Environmental Design:* The Preserve Center is LEED Platinum certified, featuring sustainable design elements and materials that reflect Rockefeller's commitment to environmental stewardship.

HISTORICAL CONTEXT: The Laurance S. Rockefeller Preserve is situated on land with a rich history. Originally the site of the valley's first dude ranch established by Lewis Joy and Struthers Burt in 1908, the land was later purchased by John D. Rockefeller, Jr. In 1990, Laurance S. Rockefeller donated approximately 2,000 acres to Grand Teton National Park, with additional land transferred in 2007 after extensive restoration efforts. The Preserve Center, dedicated in 2008, embodies Rockefeller's vision of a place where visitors can connect with nature in a serene and reflective environment.

CONTACT INFORMATION: *Address:* Moose–Wilson Rd, Grand Teton National Park, Wyoming, USA | *Phone:* 307-739-3654 | *Website: https://www.nps.gov/grte/planyourvisit/lsrpvc.htm*

BEAR AND WILDLIFE SAFETY: You should be prepared for encounters with wildlife, including black and grizzly bears. Always maintain a distance of at least 100 yards from bears and 25 yards from other wildlife. For safety tips and more information on how to stay safe in bear country, consult with park rangers.

The Laurance S. Rockefeller Preserve Center offers a peaceful retreat for nature lovers and a gateway to exploring the natural wonders of Grand Teton National Park. Whether you're visiting the exhibits, attending a ranger program, or hiking to Phelps Lake, the Preserve provides a rich and immersive experience in one of America's most beautiful landscapes.

10. COLTER BAY VILLAGE

Located along the shores of Jackson Lake, Colter Bay Village offers you services, including camping, lodging, dining, and a marina. It's an ideal starting point for exploring the park's northern region and enjoying recreational activities on the lake. When planning a family adventure in Grand Teton National Park, Colter Bay Village is an ideal destination offering a blend of historic charm, natural beauty, and a variety of outdoor activities. Located on the picturesque shores of Jackson Lake with the stunning Teton Range as a backdrop, this village provides an affordable and memorable vacation experience.

ACCOMMODATION OPTIONS IN COLTER BAY VILLAGE

CABINS: Colter Bay Village features cozy, historic mountain cabins that offer comfort and convenience. Options range from simple two-bedroom cabins to rustic tent cabins equipped with bunk beds, a wood stove, and picnic areas. Each cabin includes basic amenities like a coffee maker and comfortable bedding. The cabins maintain their historic charm while providing modern comforts such as individual room heaters and updated bathrooms.

CAMPING: If you prefer a more traditional camping experience, Colter Bay offers both tent and RV camping. All camping is by reservation only, which can be made six months in advance at Recreation.gov. The campground is well-maintained, providing a serene and natural setting for campers.

ACTIVITIES TO DO AT THE COLTER BAY VILLAGE

Colter Bay Village is often described as a summer camp for the whole family due to the wide range of activities available:

BOATING: Explore Jackson Lake by renting a canoe, kayak, or motorboat from the Colter Bay Marina. The lake is home to several islands and abundant wildlife, making for a scenic and peaceful boating experience. | **HIKING:** The area features several trails ranging from easy to moderate. Popular hikes include the Lakeshore Trail, Heron Pond and Swan Lake loop, and the longer Hermitage Point trail. These trails offer stunning views of the Teton Range and opportunities to spot wildlife. | **HORSEBACK RIDING:** Experience the park from a different perspective by taking a guided horseback ride through the surrounding wilderness. | **FISHING AND SWIMMING:** Jackson Lake is perfect for fishing enthusiasts and offers several spots for a refreshing swim during the warmer months. | **BEACH-GOING:** Relax on the lakeshore and enjoy the breathtaking views of the mountains.

VISITOR SERVICES

VISITOR CENTER: The Colter Bay Visitor Center is an excellent resource for park information. Here, you can speak with a ranger, obtain backcountry permits, and learn about the Indigenous cultures through the Indigenous Arts and Cultural Demonstration Program. The visitor center also offers exhibits and artwork for visitors to enjoy. | **DINING AND SHOPPING: Colter Bay Village has various dining options, including an on-site restaurant and a coffee bar inside the grocery store. The grocery store and gift shop provide essentials and souvenirs to make your stay comfortable.

WILDLIFE AND SAFETY

Colter Bay Village is home to diverse wildlife, including black and grizzly bears, moose, and elk. It is crucial to stay alert and follow safety guidelines: **BEAR SAFETY:** Always maintain a distance of at least 100 yards from bears and 25 yards from other wildlife. Keep your food stored securely and never approach wild animals. | **WILDLIFE VIEWING:** Dawn and dusk are the best times to observe wildlife. Popular spots for wildlife viewing include *Willow Flats Overlook* and *Oxbow Bend Turnout.*

PRACTICAL INFORMATION

RESERVATIONS: Cabin reservations can be made up to 12 months in advance online or by calling 307-543-3100. Camping reservations are available six months in advance through Recreation.gov.

LOCATION: Colter Bay Village is located in the northern part of Grand Teton National Park, along the shore of Jackson Lake. The village's address is 100 Colter Bay Village Road, Grand Teton National Park, WY 83013.

ACCESSIBILITY: The village offers reduced mobility rooms and accessible facilities. It's advisable to confirm specific needs when booking.

TIPS

Entrance Gate: There is no entrance gate when entering from Yellowstone. Visitor centers or information stations provide park maps and newspapers. | *Jackson Lake:* This natural lake also functions as a reservoir, with added storage during dry years. | *Wildlife Viewing:* Prime locations include Willow Flats Overlook and Oxbow Bend Turnout.

Colter Bay Village offers a unique and enjoyable experience for visitors of all ages, making it an excellent choice for your next family adventure in Grand Teton National Park.

TOP 10 ACTIVITIES IN GRAND TETON NATIONAL PARK

Planning a trip to Grand Teton National Park? Whether you're celebrating an anniversary, honeymoon, or simply embarking on a road trip with family or friends, this stunning park offers unforgettable experiences for everyone. Here are the top 10 activities to enjoy in Grand Teton National Park:

1. WILD & SCENIC RAFTING ON THE SNAKE RIVER

Embark on a scenic raft trip along the Snake River with an expert guide. Spot wildlife such as moose, beavers, eagles, and osprey while learning about the area's history and geology. Opt for a rafting trip that includes a freshly prepared lunch or dinner along the riverbank for a truly memorable experience. Don't forget your camera for some fantastic photos!

2. THE 42-MILE SCENIC LOOP DRIVE

Take a personal tour of the park with the 42-Mile Scenic Loop Drive. This route covers Teton Park Road, Jenny Lake Scenic Drive, and Highway 89. Key stops include Jenny Lake, Craig Thomas Visitor Center, Schwabacher's Landing, Snake River Overlook, Cunningham Cabin, and Oxbow Bend. This drive offers incredible views and numerous photo opportunities.

3. HORSEBACK RIDES

Experience the park like the early explorers by going on a horseback ride. Jackson Lake Lodge offers one and two-hour rides with views of the Tetons, Oxbow Bend, and the Snake River. At Colter Bay Village, you can enjoy rides that take you through wildflower meadows and provide panoramic mountain views.

4. HIKING

Grand Teton National Park is a hiker's paradise with trails for all skill levels. Popular short hikes include Hidden Falls, Inspiration Point, String Lake, Leigh Lake, and Swan and Heron Pond. For a more challenging full-day hike, try Cascade Canyon, Death Canyon, or

Paintbrush Canyon, where you'll encounter stunning granite peaks and remote lakes.

5. RANGER & NATURALIST PROGRAMS

Join a park ranger for guided hikes, campfire programs, or Tipi demos. At Colter Bay Village and Jackson Lake Lodge, naturalists and historians offer a variety of programs, including live raptor presentations, grizzly bear talks, and historical tours. Don't miss the Junior Ranger program, which is fun for all ages.

6. FISHING

Enjoy fly fishing or lake fishing at Jenny Lake, Jackson Lake, or the Snake River. Whether you fish on your own or with a guide, the experience is often a highlight of any visit. Guided trips include all necessary equipment, except for a fishing license, which can be purchased locally. Be sure to review the park's fishing guidelines.

7. WILDLIFE VIEWING

Grand Teton National Park offers some of the best wildlife viewing opportunities in the US. Spot bears, bison, moose, elk, pronghorn, and eagles in their natural habitats. For the best wildlife sightings, visit Willow Flats, Oxbow Bend, Elk Ranch Flats, and Moose. Check with a Visitor Center or the Jackson Lake Lodge Activity Desk for recent animal sightings.

8. BOAT RENTALS

Rent a kayak, canoe, or motorboat from Colter Bay Marina and explore Jackson Lake. Discover serene bays and islands like Colter Bay and Half Moon Bay. Boat rentals include maps, lifejackets, and radios, making for a relaxing and enjoyable morning or afternoon on the water.

9. BUS TOURS OF GRAND TETON AND YELLOWSTONE NATIONAL PARKS

A guided bus tour is a great way to get an introduction to the park. These tours offer opportunities to spot wildlife, learn about the park's history, and visit popular sites. Enjoy panoramic views of the Tetons with frequent stops to explore. A bus tour at the beginning of your trip can help you decide which areas you'd like to revisit.

10. PICNIC AND SWIM AT STRING LAKE
OR COLTER BAY SWIM BEACH

Cool off with a swim in the clear, pristine waters of String Lake or Colter Bay. Both locations offer picnic tables, grills, nearby parking, and ample shoreline for swimming and paddleboarding. Enjoy a relaxing afternoon surrounded by stunning mountain views.

Plan your visit and make the most of these incredible activities to create unforgettable memories in Grand Teton National Park!

<u>OUTDOOR ADVENTURES</u>

- Hiking

- Climbing & Mountaineering

- Wildlife Viewing

- Boating & Kayaking

- Camping

- Biking

- Photography

- Scenic Drives

- Fishing

- Rafting: Scenic Floats & Whitewater Adventures

- Visitor Centers and Interpretive Programs

HIKING: 10 BEST HIKES & TRAILS IN GRAND TETON NATIONAL PARK

1. PHELPS LAKE, LAKE CREEK, AND WOODLAND LOOP

Phelps Lake, Lake Creek, and Woodland Loop is an 11.3-km moderately challenging loop trail located near Moose, Wyoming, within Grand Teton National Park. The hike typically takes around 2 hours and 45 minutes to complete and is popular for backpacking, birding, and camping. Pets are not allowed. No reservations are needed, but there is an entrance fee. The best time to hike this trail is from May through September, with mornings being ideal to secure parking and enjoy cooler temperatures. Hikers can expect beautiful views of lakes, mountains, and wildlife such as bears, moose, and deer.

2. THE CASCADE CANYON TRAIL

The Cascade Canyon Trail is a moderately challenging 14.6 km out-and-back hike, typically completed in 3 hours and 45 minutes. The trail offers stunning views of the canyon, waterfalls, and wildlife, including moose and bears. Pets are not allowed. No reservation is needed, but an entrance fee is required. The trailhead is accessible from Jenny Lake, with a shuttle boat available for convenience. The best season to hike is June through October, with early mornings recommended to avoid crowds and see more wildlife.

3. THE DELTA LAKE VIA LUPINE MEADOWS ACCESS TRAIL

The Delta Lake via Lupine Meadows Access trail is a challenging 11.9 km out-and-back hike with a 700 m elevation gain. This unofficial, unmaintained trail features boulder fields, steep inclines, and loose dirt, requiring careful navigation. The hike typically takes several hours, depending on fitness levels. Pets are not allowed, and no reservations are needed. The trailhead is at the Lupine Meadows parking lot. The best hiking season is from May to October, with early mornings recommended to avoid crowds and enjoy cooler temperatures. The trail offers stunning views of Delta Lake, wildflowers, and wildlife, including bears.

4. HIDDEN FALLS VIA STRING LAKE TRAIL

Hidden Falls via String Lake Trail is a 7.4 km out-and-back hike Known for its stunning lake views and lush, biodiverse surroundings, this moderately challenging trail takes about 1 hour and 48 minutes to complete. Hiking is the primary activity, though running is also popular here. Pets are not allowed on this trail. No reservations are needed, but park entry fees apply. The best season to visit is from May through October, with early mornings being ideal to avoid crowds. You should be prepared for snow and muddy conditions, especially in spring.

5. THE TAGGART LAKE LOOP

The Taggart Lake Loop is a 6.1-km loop trail popular for bird watching, hiking, running, and horseback riding. The easy trail takes about 1 hour and 32 minutes to complete, offering stunning views of the Teton Range, a serene lake, and diverse biomes. Pets are not allowed. No reservations are needed, but an entrance fee applies. The best season to hike is from May through October, with early mornings being ideal to avoid crowds and mosquitoes. The trailhead is conveniently located off Teton Park Road.

6. THE BRADLEY LAKE TRAIL

The Bradley Lake Trail offers a moderately challenging 8.4 km loop with an elevation gain of 198 m, typically completed in 2 hours and 10 minutes. This popular trail is great for bird watching, hiking, and running. Pets are not allowed, and no reservations are needed. The trail provides stunning views of the Tetons, lakes, and diverse vegetation. Trekking poles are recommended, especially during snowy or muddy conditions. The best season to visit is from May through September. To avoid crowds, it's advisable to start early in the morning. Wildlife sightings, including moose and bears, are common, adding to the trail's allure.

7. JENNY LAKE TRAIL

Jenny Lake Trail is an 11.6 km loop trail near Moose, Wyoming. This moderately challenging hike offers stunning views of Jenny Lake and the Teton Range, with an average completion time of 2 hours and 31 minutes. The trail is ideal for hiking and snowshoeing, but pets are not allowed. No reservations are needed. The best time to visit is from June through October, with early morning hikes recommended to avoid crowds. To reach the trailhead, drive down Teton Park Road and turn at South Jenny Lake. Parking can be challenging, so arrive early.

8. HIDDEN FALLS VIA JENNY LAKE TRAIL

Hidden Falls via Jenny Lake Trail in Grand Teton National Park, near Moose, Wyoming, offers a scenic 7.9-km loop hike. Rated moderately challenging, it typically takes around 2 hours to complete. The trail is popular for birding, camping, and hiking, but dogs are not allowed. Reservations are not needed. The best hiking season is May through October, with early mornings recommended to avoid crowds. To reach the trail, travel north from Moose to South Jenny Lake along the Teton Park Road, and park at the Jenny Lake Visitor Center or boat dock. Consider taking the short detour to Inspiration Point for additional views.

9. THE TAGGART LAKE AND BRADLEY LAKE LOOP

The Taggart Lake and Bradley Lake Loop in Grand Teton National Park, near Moose, Wyoming, is a 9.7 km moderately challenging loop trail popular for hiking, birding, and running. The hike, which takes around 2.5 hours to complete, offers stunning views of mountains and lakes, with some uphill climbs and moderate elevation gains. Pets are not allowed on this trail, and no reservation is needed. The best season to hike is from May through September, with early morning being ideal to secure parking and avoid crowds. To get there, head to Grand Teton National Park and follow signs to the Taggart Lake trailhead. Remember to bring water and bug spray, as conditions can be sunny and buggy.

10. THE INSPIRATION POINT HIKE VIA

JENNY LAKE BOAT SHUTTLE

The Inspiration Point hike via Jenny Lake Boat Shuttle near Moose, Wyoming, is a 2.9 km out-and-back trail. Considered moderately challenging, it typically takes 57 minutes to complete. This family-friendly hike offers stunning views of Jenny Lake, Hidden Falls, and the Tetons, with an elevation gain of 128 meters. Pets are not allowed on this trail. Reservations are not needed, but early arrival is advised as parking is limited. The best time to hike is May through October, ideally early in the morning or late in the afternoon to avoid crowds. Access the trail by taking the boat shuttle across Jenny Lake.

CLIMBING AND MOUNTAINEERING

Rock climbing in Jackson Hole and Grand Teton National Park offers a variety of experiences, from beginner-friendly routes to challenging climbs for advanced climbers. Here are some of the top spots to try rock climbing in this beautiful area:

JACKSON HOLE MOUNTAIN RESORT

1. **CORBET'S COULOIR: Access:** Take the Aerial Tram from Jackson Hole Mountain Resort. | **Climbs:** Bolted climbs ranging from 5.10 to 5.13. | **Experience:** Unique approach via tram with stunning views of the Tetons. Impress passengers with your climbing skills.

2. **VIA FERRATA: Location:** Jackson Hole Mountain Resort. | **Description:** An outdoor climbing course designed for beginners. Work with a guide to scale bridges and walls. | **Experience:** Safe, guided introduction to climbing, suitable for families and beginners.

GRAND TETON NATIONAL PARK

3. **BLACK TAIL BUTTE: Location:** Inside Grand Teton National Park. | *Climbs:* A mix of hard sport climbs and easier routes close to the parking lot. | **Experience:** Majestic location with views of the Grand Teton. Great for photography and enjoying the natural beauty.

4. **GUIDE'S WALL:** *Access:* Hike 5 miles around Jenny Lake or take the Jenny Lake Ferry to save time. | *Climb**:* 800-foot multi-pitch climb with several variations. | *Experience:* Classic climb in the park with a mix of easy and challenging pitches. Scenic views from Cascade Canyon.

NEAR JACKSON HOLE

5. **RODEO WALL:** *Location:* Near Hoback Junction. | *Climbs:* Mellow climbs up to 5.11. | *Experience**:* Scenic spot near the Snake River, popular with rafters. Features notable climbs like "Time Flies While You're Alive In Wyoming."

DOWNTOWN JACKSON

6. **BOULDERING WALL AT SNOW KING MOUNTAIN:** *Location:* Teton Boulder Park at the base of Snow King Mountain. | *Description:*

Outdoor bouldering wall with various routes. | *Experience:* Free and fun, family-friendly activity with nearby picnic areas and other recreational options like the Cowboy Coaster and Treetop Adventure course.

THE GRAND TETON

7. CLIMBING THE GRAND TETON: Iconic climb with routes such as the Exum Ridge. | *Experience:* Suitable for climbers of various skill levels, though guided tours are recommended for beginners. A monumental adventure with breathtaking views. | *Guides:* Exum Mountain Guides.

ADDITIONAL INFORMATION

Safety: Always prioritize safety, especially in alpine environments. Consider hiring a guide if you are unfamiliar with the area or new to climbing. | **Preparation:** Proper physical conditioning and familiarity with climbing techniques are essential, particularly for more challenging routes like the Grand Teton. | **Gear:** Ensure you have the appropriate climbing gear and check local regulations and weather conditions before heading out.

These climbing spots provide a range of options to suit different skill levels and offer incredible experiences in the stunning landscapes of Jackson Hole and Grand Teton National Park.

WILDLIFE VIEWING

Grand Teton National Park hosts a remarkable array of wildlife, including iconic species such as grizzly bears, black bears, bison, moose, elk, pronghorn antelope, wolves, and a variety of bird species like bald eagles, ospreys, and trumpeter swans. Each species has unique habitat requirements, from the rivers and lakes to the sagebrush flats and dense forests, offering visitors different opportunities for observation throughout the park.

TOP WILDLIFE VIEWING AREAS

1. MOOSE-WILSON ROAD: Known for its beaver ponds and willow marshes, this area is excellent for spotting moose and bears, especially during the early morning or at dusk when wildlife tends to be more active.

2. ANTELOPE FLATS: Home to vast sagebrush plains, this area is ideal for viewing bison and pronghorn antelope. The open landscape also attracts predators such as coyotes and birds of prey.

3. OXBOW BEND: Along the Snake River, Oxbow Bend is famous for its scenic vistas and diverse wildlife. Visitors can often observe moose grazing along the water's edge, bald eagles soaring overhead, and river otters playing in the slow-moving water.

4. WILLOW FLATS: Particularly active during the elk calving season (mid-May to mid-June), Willow Flats provides excellent opportunities to see elk and sometimes bears searching for prey. It's also a haven for birdwatchers, with species like pelicans and herons frequenting the area.

BEST PRACTICES FOR WILDLIFE VIEWING

MAINTAIN A SAFE DISTANCE: It's crucial to respect wildlife and their habitats by keeping a safe distance. This means staying at least 100 yards away from bears and wolves, and at least 25 yards from all other wildlife.

USE BINOCULARS AND CAMERAS: Binoculars, spotting scopes, and telephoto lenses are essential tools for observing wildlife up close without disturbing them. This approach ensures both your safety and the animals' well-being.

BE RESPECTFUL: Avoid approaching or disturbing animals, especially mothers with young. Wildlife can become stressed or aggressive if they feel threatened or cornered.

STAY INFORMED: Ranger-led programs and visitor centers offer valuable insights into wildlife behavior and the best viewing locations. Understanding each species' habits and preferred habitats enhances the likelihood of meaningful wildlife encounters.

RESPONSIBLE BEHAVIOR: Refrain from feeding wildlife or leaving food accessible, as this disrupts natural behaviors and can harm animals in the long term.

Grand Teton National Park provides an exceptional opportunity to witness wildlife in its natural habitat, offering breathtaking scenery and diverse ecosystems. By following guidelines for responsible wildlife viewing and exploring designated areas, visitors can experience the beauty and majesty of North American wildlife while contributing to conservation efforts to protect these precious species for future generations.

RAFTING, BOATING AND KAYAKING

RAFTING: SCENIC FLOATS & WHITEWATER ADVENTURES

Experience Grand Teton National Park from a unique perspective by rafting on the scenic Snake River. With options ranging from calm scenic floats to thrilling whitewater adventures, there's something for everyone.

SCENIC FLOAT TRIPS

Mad River Rafting offers serene 10-mile floats on the Snake River, perfect for observing the park's natural beauty and wildlife. For more details, visit *https://mad-river.com*.

Barker-Ewing Scenic Float Trips has been guiding trips since 1963, providing knowledgeable guides to help you spot moose, beavers, eagles, and even the occasional wolf or bear. Learn more at *https://barkerewing.com*.

Solitude Float Trips offers 2-hour floats suitable for families and photographers. Multiple departures throughout the day provide flexibility. Find more info at *https://grand-teton-scenic-floats.com*.

Grand Teton Lodge Company also offers 10-mile non-whitewater floats with options for lunch or dinner trips. More information can be found at *https://www.gtlc.com/activities/rafting-the-snake-river*.

WHITEWATER RAFTING

For those seeking excitement, **Mad River Boat Trips** provides whitewater adventures with various boat sizes for different thrill levels. Check out their offerings at *https://mad-river.com*.

Jackson Hole Whitewater has been operating for over 50 years, offering thrilling whitewater experiences on the Snake River. Visit *https://jhww.com* for more information.

BOATING IN GRAND TETON NATIONAL PARK

Boating on Jackson and Jenny Lakes offers stunning views and serene waters. Both motorized and non-motorized vessels are allowed, and sailboats are welcome on Jackson Lake. Here's what you need to know:

RENTALS

Colter Bay Marina offers rentals for various watercraft. For details, visit *https://www.gtlc.com/activities/marina-slip-and-buoy-rentals.*
Jenny Lake Boating provides boat rentals and other water activities. More information is available at *https://jennylakeboating.com/boat-trips/rental-boats.*
Signal Mountain Marina also offers a variety of boat rentals. Learn more at *https://www.signalmountainlodge.com/lodge-services/boat-rentals.*

PERMITS AND REGULATIONS

A Grand Teton Boat Permit is required for all vessels, which can be purchased online at Recreation.gov or at park visitor centers.
Wyoming AIS Decal is mandatory to prevent the spread of aquatic invasive species. Decals can be purchased from the Wyoming Game and Fish Department.
Ensure compliance with safety equipment regulations, including personal flotation devices, navigation lights, fire extinguishers, and signaling devices.

KAYAKING AND CANOEING

For those who enjoy paddling, Grand Teton National Park offers beautiful settings for kayaking and canoeing:

RENTALS AND LOCATIONS

Colter Bay Village Marina offers rentals on a first-come, first-served basis. Visit *https://www.gtlc.com/activities/kayak-canoe-motorboat-rentals* for more details.
Enjoy paddling on the Snake River or clear lakes within the park for stunning views, world-class fishing, and wildlife sightings.

SAFETY AND PERMITS

Obtain a Grand Teton Boat Permit and Wyoming AIS Decal before launching. Follow safety guidelines, including wearing personal flotation devices and understanding local watercraft regulations.

Whether you prefer the calm of a scenic float, the thrill of whitewater rafting, or the serenity of kayaking, Grand Teton National Park offers a variety of water activities to help you beat the summer heat and enjoy the stunning natural beauty.

CAMPING

Grand Teton National Park offers a spectacular camping experience with its incredible views, fresh mountain air, and diverse campgrounds. To ensure you make the most of your visit, it's essential to plan ahead, especially now that all campsites require reservations. This guide provides detailed information on the various campgrounds, RV parks, and facilities within the park, along with tips for a successful camping trip.

CAMPGROUND OVERVIEW

1. COLTER BAY CAMPGROUND: *Location:* 25 miles north of Moose | **Open:** Mid-May to late-September | **Sites:** 335 sites, 11 group sites, 13 electric hookup site | **Amenities:** Showers, laundry, trailer dump station | **Phone:** 307-543-3100 | **Details:** Nestled in a wooded area near Jackson Lake, this campground is suitable for tents, trailers, and RVs. It offers easy access to various activities and scenic views.

2. GROS VENTRE CAMPGROUND: Location: 11.5 miles south and east of Moose | **Open:** Early-May to early-October | **Sites:** Over 300 sites, 5 group sites, 36 electric hookup sites | **Amenities**: Trailer dump station | **Phone:** 307-543-3100 | **Details:** Situated along the Gros Ventre River, this campground offers a mix of sagebrush and cottonwood sites, ideal for those seeking a blend of nature and convenience.

3. HEADWATERS CAMPGROUND AND RV SITES AT FLAGG RANCH: Location: Just south of Yellowstone National Park's south boundary | **Open:** Early-June to late-September | *Sites:* 175 spacious sites, full hook-up RV sites, camper cabins | *Amenities:* Dump station, showers, laundry | **Phone:** 1-800-443-2311 | *Details:* Located in a spruce-fir forest, this campground is perfect for visitors exploring both Grand Teton and Yellowstone National Parks.

4. JENNY LAKE CAMPGROUND: *Location:* 8 miles north of Moose | *Open:* Early-May to late-September | *Sites:* 49 tent-only sites | *Phone:* 307-543-3100 | *Details:* Known for its scenic beauty, this tents-only campground offers proximity to Jenny Lake and popular hiking trails. Limited to one vehicle per site, with strict size restrictions.

5. LIZARD CREEK CAMPGROUND: Location: 32 miles north of Moose | Open: Mid-June to early-September | **Sites:** 60 sites | **Phone:** 1-800-672-6012 | **Details:** A less developed campground on the north shore of Jackson Lake, offering a more secluded experience. Suitable for tents and non-electric RVs up to 30 feet.

6. SIGNAL MOUNTAIN CAMPGROUND: Location: 9 miles north of Jenny Lake | **Open:** Mid-May to mid-October | **Sites:** 81 sites, 24 electric hookup sites | **Amenities:** Trailer dump station | **Phone**: 1-800-672-6012 | **Details:** Offering a mix of forest and lakeside sites, this campground provides stunning views and is close to Signal Mountain Lodge and marina.

RV PARKS

1. COLTER BAY RV PARK: Details: 112 sites with full hookups, showers, and laundry. | *Phone:* 307-543-3100

2. HEADWATERS CAMPGROUND AND RV SITES: Details: 100 trailer sites with full hookups, showers, and laundry. | **Phone:** 1-800-443-2311

3. GROUP CAMPING: Locations: Colter Bay and Gros Ventre campgrounds | **Capacity:** 10 to 100 people | **Reservations:** Required through the Grand Teton Lodge Company at 307-543-3100.

BACKCOUNTRY CAMPING

If you seek a more rugged experience, backcountry camping is available with necessary permits. Detailed planning is required to ensure compliance with park regulations.

ADDITIONAL FACILITIES: Showers and Laundry: Available at Colter Bay Village and Signal Mountain Lodge. | **Equipment Rentals:** Available from Teton Mountaineering, Teton Backcountry Rentals, and Skinny Skis.

RESERVATION TIPS: Create an account at recreation.gov in advance. | Reservations open six months in advance at 8:00 a.m. MST. | Log in early to increase your chances of securing a site.**

Camping in Grand Teton National Park offers a chance to immerse yourself in nature's beauty. Whether you choose a well-equipped RV site or a secluded tent spot, planning ahead and following park guidelines will ensure a memorable and enjoyable experience. Happy camping!

BIKING

Biking in Grand Teton National Park is a delightful experience that combines the thrill of cycling with the breathtaking beauty of the Teton Range. Whether you are an expert cyclist or a beginner, the park offers diverse pathways and roads to explore. Here's everything you need to know to make the most of your biking adventure in Grand Teton.

THE GRAND TETON PATHWAY

The Grand Teton Pathway is a multi-use trail perfect for biking, walking, and riding at the base of the Tetons. This pathway extends from the town of Jackson, north to Antelope Flats Road, and from Moose Junction to Jenny Lake. Along the route, six hubs—Gros Ventre Roundabout, Blacktail Butte, Dornans, Moose, Taggart Lake, and Jenny Lake—offer parking and bike racks.

This pathway is open seasonally, generally from after the snow melts and park maintenance workers have swept the path. However, the section along the National Elk Refuge is closed from November 1 to April 30 due to elk migration. The pathway is part of an extensive system through Jackson and Teton County, providing a scenic and safe route for all cyclists.

ROAD BIKING IN GRAND TETON

Cycling is allowed on all paved roads within the park, as well as on the gravel Two Ocean Lake Road and Grassy Lake Road. A notable stretch is the Teton Park Road, closed to vehicles between the Taggart Lake Trailhead and Signal Mountain from November 1 to May 1, making it a cyclist's paradise when clear of snow.

While biking on roads without shoulders or with narrow shoulders, extreme caution is necessary. Always ride in the direction of traffic, in a single file line, and stay alert for vehicles, wildlife, and other cyclists.

BIKING ESSENTIALS AND SAFETY TIPS

BIKING ESSENTIALS

Food and Water: Carry at least two liters of water and high-energy snacks. | **First Aid:** A basic first aid kit is crucial. | **Layers:** Weather can change quickly; be prepared. | **Helmet:** Always wear a helmet and bright colors. | **Repair Kit:** Carry tools for minor repairs.

SAFETY TIPS

- Use hand signals to communicate with drivers.
- Maintain control of your speed.
- Never leave food unattended.
- Keep a safe distance from wildlife: 25 yards from bison, elk, and moose, and 100 yards from bears and wolves.
- Follow specific safety considerations for e-bikes, including careful mounting and dismounting due to their weight.

BICYCLE REGULATIONS

Cyclists must obey the same rules as motorized vehicles. E-bikes are considered bicycles if they have fully operable pedals and an electric motor of less than 750 watts. Bicycles are only allowed on paved and unpaved roads and designated pathways, not on hiking trails or in backcountry areas. Riding abreast of another bike is prohibited on park roads; single-file riding is mandatory. Visibility gear is required during low visibility and nighttime. A park entry fee applies to cyclists.

PATHWAY HIGHLIGHTS AND BIKE RENTALS

MOOSE TO JENNY LAKE: A 23-mile round trip offering stunning views and a boat cruise on Jenny Lake.

JACKSON TO MOOSE: A 29-mile round trip featuring stops at the National Museum of Wildlife Art and Dornan's for lunch.

WILSON TO TETON VILLAGE: A 17-mile round trip including a scenic ride and lunch options in Teton Village.

Bike rentals are available throughout Jackson Hole, with shops like Hoback Sports, Teton Mountain Bike Tours, Wilson Backcountry Sports, and Jackson Hole Sports providing rentals and guided tours. For convenience, consider the START Bike community bike share program in Jackson.

EXPLORING JACKSON HOLE PATHWAYS

Jackson Hole is renowned for its bike-friendly pathways, with over 70 miles of multi-use trails. These pathways offer smooth rides with stunning Teton views and are accessible for all skill levels. In winter, some pathways are groomed for cross-country skiing and snowshoeing, making them a year-round attraction.

From leisurely rides to challenging routes, biking in Grand Teton National Park and Jackson Hole is an exhilarating way to immerse yourself in nature and enjoy the majestic landscapes of this beautiful region. Whether you're seeking a family outing or a solo adventure, the pathways and road biking opportunities in Grand Teton offer something for everyone.

PHOTOGRAPHY

Grand Teton National Park is a photographer's paradise, offering a diverse range of stunning landscapes & abundant wildlife. Whether you're a seasoned professional or a passionate amateur, the park provides endless opportunities to capture breathtaking images throughout the year.

TOP PHOTOGRAPHY LOCATIONS IN
GRAND TETON NATIONAL PARK

1. SCHWABACHER'S LANDING: Schwabacher's Landing is a top favorite among photographers, offering spectacular reflections of the Teton Range in the calm waters of the Snake River. Arrive early to capture the first light of dawn and explore the riverbank for unique angles. Don't forget to bring river sandals to venture into the water for more creative shots. | **2. MORMON ROW AND MOULTON BARN:** Located on Antelope Flats, the historic Mormon Row features the iconic T.A. Moulton Barn, one of the most photographed barns in the world. If you're lucky, you might also capture a herd of bison grazing in the foreground. Visit during the early morning or late evening for the best lighting conditions. | **3. OXBOW BEND OF THE SNAKE RIVER:** Oxbow Bend is another fantastic location for reflections, particularly of Mount Moran. The best time to visit is early morning before the wind disturbs the water's surface. Explore the riverbank to find the perfect frame, and don't hesitate to climb to higher vantage points for panoramic shots. | **4. SNAKE RIVER OVERLOOK:** Made famous by Ansel Adams, the Snake River Overlook provides a classic view of the winding river with the Tetons in the background. Though trees have grown since Adams' time, this spot still offers iconic views, especially at sunrise. Arrive early to secure your spot and enjoy the camaraderie of fellow photographers. | **5. WILDFLOWER FIELDS:** In late spring and early summer, fields of wildflowers bloom across the park. Antelope Flats is a prime location, offering a mix of wildflowers, wildlife, and historic buildings. For more floral diversity, explore the river bottoms near Schwabacher's Landing and Oxbow Bend, where you can find Indian Paintbrush and lupine.

PRO TIPS FOR PHOTOGRAPHING IN GRAND TETON

PLAN FOR SUNRISE AND SUNSET: The "magic" light occurs when the sun rises or sets, reflecting off clouds over the Tetons. Clear skies to the east and incoming weather from the west create stunning light conditions. Use a split neutral density filter to balance the exposure between the bright mountains and the darker valley. | **DRESS APPROPRIATELY:** Layer up, as temperatures can vary widely. A down jacket is useful year-round. | **STAY SAFE AND RESPECT WILDLIFE:** Always maintain a safe distance from animals, and carry bear spray. Avoid disturbing wildlife for the perfect shot. Use a telephoto lens and extenders to capture close-up images without getting too close. | **BE SOCIAL:** Engage with fellow photographers. Sharing tips and experiences can enhance your visit and lead to new perspectives. Use the hashtag #OnlyinJH to share your photos and find inspiration from others.

ADDITIONAL RESOURCES AND INSPIRATION

MANGELSEN - IMAGES OF NATURE GALLERY: Visit Tom Mangelsen's gallery in Jackson for inspiration and to see works from one of the most influential nature photographers. | **WILD BY NATURE PHOTOGRAPHY GALLERY:** Featuring Henry H. Holdsworth's stunning wildlife and landscape photography, this gallery is a must-visit in Jackson. | Grand Teton National Park offers a wealth of photographic opportunities that can inspire and challenge photographers of all levels.

SCENIC DRIVES

Grand Teton National Park is renowned for its stunning landscapes, and one of the best ways to experience its beauty is through its scenic drives. Here are some of the most notable routes you can explore:

1. **MOOSE-WILSON ROAD:** The Moose-Wilson Road is a corridor connecting the towns of Moose and Wilson. This 7-mile road follows the Snake River and is excellent for wildlife viewing. However, be aware that the southern portion of Moose-Wilson Road between Granite Canyon Entrance and the LSR Preserve is under construction in 2023, with possible 20-minute delays. | **Type:** Scenic Driving | **Duration:** 20-60 Minutes | **Location:** Moose-Wilson **Season:** Spring, Summer, Fall

2. **JENNY LAKE SCENIC DRIVE:** The Jenny Lake Scenic Drive skirts the east shore of Jenny Lake, offering spectacular views of the Teton peaks. This drive is particularly beautiful during the fall when the leaves are changing colors. | Type: Scenic Driving | Duration: 15-30 Minutes | Location: Jenny Lake | Season: Spring, Summer, Fall

3. **SIGNAL MOUNTAIN SUMMIT ROAD:** The Signal Mountain Summit Road features exhilarating switchbacks and climbs 1,000 feet to an observation area. From the summit, you can enjoy panoramic views of the Teton Range and Jackson Hole. | **Type:** Scenic Driving | **Duration:** 30-60 Minutes | **Location:** Signal Mountain | **Season:** Spring, Summer, Fall

4. **TETON PARK ROAD:** The Teton Park Road is a well-maintained paved road that follows the base of the Teton Range from Moose to Jackson Lake Junction. This road offers stunning views of the mountains and access to many of the park's main attractions. | **Type:** Scenic Driving | **Duration:** 30-60 Minutes | **Location:** Moose–Jackson Lake Junction | **Season:** Spring, Summer, Fall

ADDITIONAL SCENIC ROUTES

Buffalo Valley: This partially paved road offers views of the Buffalo Fork River against the backdrop of the Tetons.

Grassy Lake Road: An unpaved road leading through deep backcountry to Idaho.

Gros Ventre Road: This road follows the Gros Ventre River, leading to camping spots, trailheads, and popular whitewater rafting and kayaking areas.

Highway 191: The main highway connecting travelers to major towns and attractions around the park.

Jenny Lake Loop A 5-mile one-way road offering views of the cathedral group of the Tetons and Jenny Lake.

Kelly WY & Antelope Flats: A scenic drive through sage-covered Antelope Flats, perfect for viewing elk and buffalo.

Rockefeller Parkway: This road links Grand Teton and Yellowstone National Parks, providing good opportunities for wildlife spotting.

SAFETY TIPS

While driving through Grand Teton National Park, always watch for large animals on the road, especially at night when visibility is low. The speed limit on US Highway 26/89/191 is 45 mph from 30 minutes after sunset to 30 minutes before sunrise. Wearing your seatbelt and driving carefully protects both you and the wildlife.

MAPS AND FURTHER INFORMATION

For more detailed information and maps, check the Grand Teton National Park website: *https://www.nps.gov/grte/index.htm*. Enjoy your scenic drive and the breathtaking views that Grand Teton National Park has to offer!

FISHING

Among the diverse range of outdoor activities to do in Grand Teton National Park, fishing stands out as a popular pursuit for both seasoned anglers and casual enthusiasts alike. With its crystal-clear lakes, pristine rivers, and abundant fish populations, the park offers a fishing experience that is both rewarding and unforgettable.

PRIME FISHING LOCATIONS

Grand Teton National Park boasts a variety of fishing spots catering to different preferences. *Jackson Lake*, the largest lake in the park, is a favorite among anglers seeking lake trout, cutthroat trout, and Mackinaw. *Jenny Lake*, smaller and more intimate, provides opportunities to catch cutthroat and lake trout amidst stunning mountain vistas. *Phelps Lake*, accessible via a scenic hike, is known for its seclusion and healthy populations of cutthroat trout. *The Snake River,* flowing through the park, is a renowned fly-fishing destination. Anglers can wade in its waters or embark on guided float trips to Target cutthroat trout and other species. Tributaries like the *Gros Ventre River* also offer exciting fishing opportunities, particularly if you seek brook trout. For the adventurous, the park's backcountry hides numerous alpine lakes and streams teeming with fish. These remote locations require more effort to reach but reward anglers with solitude and pristine fishing grounds. | **Lewis Lake and Lewis River:** Located in Yellowstone, these areas are great for both novice and experienced anglers, offering brown, brook, and lake trout ranging from 16-24 inches. The serene setting and drift boat float trips are highlights. | **Firehole River:** Known for intermediate to advanced wade fishing amid Yellowstone's geysers and buffalo. Anglers can catch rainbow, brown, and brook trout. | **Green and New Fork Rivers**:** Famous for adventurous fishing trips and large trout (brown, rainbow, and cutthroat) often exceeding 20 inches. Wildlife sightings include moose and cowboys. | **Snake River**:** Flowing through Grand Teton National Park, home to the native Snake River Cutthroat Trout and part of the U.S. Wild and Scenic Rivers program, offering excellent fishing opportunities. | **Salt River:** A tributary of the Snake River, ideal for escaping crowds with cold, clear waters housing fine-spotted cutthroat and brown trout. Dry fly fishing is particularly productive during insect hatches. | **Bighorn River:** Near Thermopolis, Wyoming, this blue-ribbon trout fishery is known for trophy trout and is ideal for challenging fishing, with brown, rainbow, and cutthroat trout. | **Flat Creek:** Located on the National Elk Refuge, it offers large, elusive trout for advanced anglers and relaxed wade fishing south of Jackson. | **Yellowstone Lake:** Known for large cutthroat trout, providing a rewarding fishing experience. Remote areas accessible by powerboat hold more fish and offer a serene environment.

DIVERSE FISH SPECIES

Grand Teton National Park's waters are home to a diverse array of fish species. The *Snake River cutthroat trout*, a native species, is a prized catch for many anglers. *Rainbow trout*, *brook trout*, and *brown trout* are also present, adding to the variety. *Lake trout*, known for their size and fighting spirit, are sought after in the park's deeper lakes. *Mountain whitefish*, though less targeted, provide additional sport for anglers.

FISHING REGULATIONS AND CONSERVATION

To ensure the sustainability of fish populations, Grand Teton National Park has established fishing regulations that anglers must adhere to. A valid Wyoming fishing license is required, and catch-and-release practices are often encouraged, especially for native species like the Snake River cutthroat trout. Seasonal restrictions may apply to protect spawning fish, so it's essential to check the park's regulations before casting a line.

TECHNIQUES AND TIPS

Fly fishing is the preferred method in many of the park's waters, particularly in the Snake River. Anglers can use dry flies, nymphs, or streamers depending on the season and conditions. Spin fishing is also popular in lakes and some rivers, with lures like spoons, spinners, and Rapalas proving effective. Bait fishing is allowed in specific areas, with worms and salmon eggs being common choices. *The best times to fish in Grand Teton National Park vary* depending on the species and location. Generally, spring and fall offer excellent fishing conditions as the water temperatures are moderate and fish are more active. Summer can also be productive, especially early mornings and evenings when the sun is less intense.

CONSERVATION EFFORTS

Grand Teton National Park is committed to preserving its natural resources, including its fish populations. The park actively monitors fish health and populations, implements habitat restoration projects, and partners with organizations to promote responsible fishing practices. Anglers are encouraged to participate in these efforts by following regulations, practicing catch-and-release, and respecting the delicate ecosystem.

FISHING SERVICES AND AMENITIES

The park offers a range of services to enhance the fishing experience. Guided fishing trips are available from licensed outfitters who provide expert knowledge of local waters, techniques, and regulations. Local fishing shops offer gear rentals and purchases, ensuring that anglers have everything they need for a successful outing. Numerous lodging options are available, ranging from campgrounds to luxurious resorts, allowing visitors to choose accommodations that suit their preferences and budgets.

PERSONAL EXPERIENCES AND STORIES

Countless anglers have found solace and excitement while fishing in Grand Teton National Park. Stories abound of epic battles with trophy trout, peaceful mornings on serene lakes, and the camaraderie forged between fishing companions. These personal experiences contribute to the park's allure and inspire others to embark on their own fishing adventures.

Grand Teton National Park offers a fishing experience that is as diverse as its landscape. Whether you're a seasoned angler seeking a challenge or a novice eager to cast your first line, the park's abundant waters and diverse fish species promise a rewarding adventure. By respecting the park's regulations and practicing responsible fishing, you can contribute to the preservation of this natural treasure for generations to come. So pack your gear, grab your fishing license, and embark on a journey to experience the thrill of fishing in Grand Teton National Park, where nature's bounty awaits.

VISITOR CENTERS &
INTERPRETIVE PROGRAMS

Craig Thomas visitor center in Grand Teton National Park

1. THE CRAIG THOMAS DISCOVERY & VISITOR CENTER

The Craig Thomas Discovery & Visitor Center, located in Grand Teton National Park, offers a rich experience reflecting the area's natural beauty and cultural heritage. Positioned 12 miles north of Jackson, Wyoming, at 100 Discovery Way, Moose, it provides essential resources for visitors, including trip planning, backcountry or boating permits, and a Grand Teton Association Park Store. Open daily from 8:00 AM to 5:00 PM in summer, with varied hours in spring and fall, the center closes from November 1 to April 30. Inside, you can explore exhibits on the Teton Range, mountaineering, and Indigenous tribes, enhancing their understanding of the region's past, present, and future. Amenities include bear canister and spray rentals, a theater, accessible restrooms, WiFi, water bottle filling stations, and wheelchair availability. Visitors can also attend ranger programs and watch informative movies about the park. For more information, contact the center at (307) 739-3399.

2. THE LAURANCE S. ROCKEFELLER PRESERVE CENTER

The Laurance S. Rockefeller Preserve Center in Grand Teton National Park is a hub for visitors to explore Laurance S. Rockefeller's legacy of conservation. The center features exhibits that engage the senses, including a poem by Terry Tempest Williams, audio recordings of Rockefeller, videos, photography, and a soundscape room. Visitors can relax in the resource room, participate in ranger programs, or hike to Phelps Lake. Located at 9001 Moose-Wilson Road, Moose, WY, the center is not accessible to vehicles over 23.3 feet long or trailers. The Preserve is open daily from 9:00 AM to 5:00 PM during summer, with closures during winter from September 26 to June 2 and on major holidays. Access may be impacted by Moose-Wilson Road construction in 2022. For more information, contact the center at (307) 739-3654.

3. JENNY LAKE VISITOR CENTER

The Jenny Lake Visitor Center, housed in a cabin built by Harrison Crandall in 1921, celebrates art in Grand Teton National Park through Crandall's work and that of other artists. Located at 403 South Jenny Lake Dr., Moose, WY, the center includes a bookstore operated by the Grand Teton Association, ranger programs, and serves as a starting point for backcountry adventures. Rangers are available for trip planning and information both in the plaza and on trails. Nearby, the Jenny Lake Ranger Station offers backcountry permits. Open daily from 9:00 AM to 5:00 PM during summer, the center is closed from September 26 to May 11 and on major holidays. For directions, turn west at Moose Junction from Jackson and head eight miles north to Jenny Lake Junction. From Yellowstone, turn southwest at Jackson Lake Junction and drive 12 miles south. For more information, contact the center at (307) 739-3343.

4. COLTER BAY VISITOR CENTER

The Colter Bay Visitor Center, a surviving Mission 66 structure, offers stunning views of Jackson Lake in Grand Teton National Park. Located at 640 Cottonwood Way, Moran, WY, it is home to the Indigenous Arts and Cultural Demonstration Program, showcasing Indigenous art and hosting artists. Visitors can watch the park film in the auditorium, obtain trip planning information, and secure backcountry or boating permits. The center also features a Grand Teton Association bookstore and nearby shops and restaurants. Open daily from 8:00 AM to 5:00 PM during summer and 9:00 AM to 5:00 PM from May 3 to June 4, the center closes for winter from October 3 to May 2 and on major holidays. Directions include turning west at the Colter Bay Village sign, 10.5 miles north of Moran Junction on US 89/191/287, or 18.5 miles south of Yellowstone National Park. For more information, contact (307) 739-3594.

5. FLAGG RANCH INFORMATION STATION

The Flagg Ranch Information Station, located within the John D. Rockefeller, Jr. Memorial Parkway, serves as a key gateway to the Greater Yellowstone Ecosystem. Situated at 701 Flagg Drive, Moran, WY, this small wooden cabin is the first stop for visitors traveling south from Yellowstone National Park. Open daily from 9:00 AM to 3:30 PM during the peak summer season, the station provides essential trip planning information, exhibits, and restrooms. To reach Flagg Ranch, head two miles south from Yellowstone's South Gate on US 89/191/287 and turn right at the Headwaters sign. From the south, drive 22 miles north from Jackson Lake Junction and turn left at the Headwaters sign. The station is closed during winter from September 2 to June 13 and on major holidays. For more details, contact (307) 543-2372.

6. NATIONAL ELK REFUGE & GREATER YELLOWSTONE VISITOR CENTER

The National Elk Refuge & Greater Yellowstone Visitor Center, located at 532 N Cache St, Jackson, WY, is operated by the U.S. Fish and Wildlife Service on the National Elk Refuge. This inter-agency center is a collaborative hub for six agencies: Bridger-Teton National Forest, Grand Teton Association, Grand Teton National Park, National Elk Refuge, Jackson Hole Chamber of Commerce, and Wyoming Game & Fish. The center provides historical and interpretive exhibits, maps, and ranger-led information, along with amenities such as accessible restrooms and wheelchair access. Open daily from 9:00 AM to 5:00 PM, it is closed on Thanksgiving and Christmas. The visitor center serves as an essential resource for information on the Greater Yellowstone Ecosystem and trip planning. For more information, contact the center at (307) 739-9378 or visit in person.

CHAPTER 5: ITINERARY

- Adjustable 3-days Itinerary For Visiting Yellowstone & Grand Teton national parks

- Best 2-Day Yellowstone National Park Itinerary

- 3-Day Grand Teton Itinerary for Hiking Enthusiasts

ADJUSTABLE 3-DAYS ITINERARY FOR VISITING YELLOWSTONE & GRAND TETON NATIONAL PARKS

DAY 1: EXPLORE YELLOWSTONE NATIONAL PARK

6:00 AM - ENTER YELLOWSTONE NATIONAL PARK THROUGH THE WEST ENTRANCE: Arrive early to beat the crowds and maximize your day.

7:00 AM - UPPER GEYSER BASIN: Head straight to the Upper Geyser Basin to witness the eruption of Old Faithful. The geyser erupts approximately every 90 minutes. | Explore the surrounding geysers and hot springs, including Castle Geyser, Grand Geyser, and the Morning Glory Pool.

9:30 AM - GRAND PRISMATIC SPRING: Drive to the Midway Geyser Basin and take the boardwalk trail to the Grand Prismatic Spring. Spend time admiring its vibrant colors and unique formations from the boardwalk. For a better view, hike the short trail to the Grand Prismatic Overlook.

11:30 AM - NORRIS GEYSER BASIN: Continue to Norris Geyser Basin, known for its active geysers and steam vents. | Explore the Porcelain Basin and Back Basin areas. Don't miss the Steamboat Geyser, which is the tallest active geyser in the world.

1:00 PM - LUNCH BREAK: Have a picnic lunch at one of the designated picnic areas or enjoy a meal at the nearby Norris Geyser Basin Museum and Information Station.

2:00 PM - YELLOWSTONE GRAND CANYON: Drive to the Yellowstone Grand Canyon area. | Visit the Artist Point for a spectacular view of the Lower Falls and the colorful canyon walls. | Take short hikes or walk along the canyon rim for different viewpoints, such as the Brink of the Lower Falls Trail and the Lookout Point Trail.

5:00 PM - RELAXATION AND EVENING ACTIVITIES: Check into your lodge or campground and relax after a day of exploration. |

Enjoy dinner at one of the park's lodges or prepare a meal at your campsite. | Spend the evening stargazing or attending a ranger-led program if available.

DAY 2: GRAND TETON NATIONAL PARK

7:00 AM - DRIVE TO GRAND TETON NATIONAL PARK: Start your day early and head south towards Grand Teton National Park.

8:30 AM - TETON PARK ROAD: Drive along the Teton Park Road, stopping at scenic viewpoints such as Snake River Overlook and Schwabacher Landing. | Take time to capture photos and enjoy the breathtaking views of the Teton Range.

10:00 AM - JENNY LAKE: Arrive at Jenny Lake and take a boat ride across the lake. | Hike to Hidden Falls (1 mile round trip) and Inspiration Point (2 miles round trip) for stunning vistas of the lake and surrounding mountains.

12:00 PM - LUNCH BREAK: Enjoy a picnic lunch by Jenny Lake or visit the Jenny Lake Visitor Center for dining options.

1:00 PM - SIGNAL MOUNTAIN: Drive to Signal Mountain for panoramic views of the Teton Range and Jackson Hole Valley. | Take the short drive up Signal Mountain Summit Road for a stunning overlook.

2:30 PM - LAURANCE S. ROCKEFELLER PRESERVE: Visit the Laurance S. Rockefeller Preserve. | Take a leisurely hike along one of the nature trails, such as the Phelps Lake Loop Trail, and learn about the park's ecology and conservation efforts.

4:30 PM - WILDLIFE VIEWING: Spend the late afternoon exploring the park's wildlife-rich areas, such as Moose-Wilson Road and Antelope Flats. | Keep an eye out for moose, elk, bison, and other wildlife.

6:00 PM - EVENING RELAXATION: Enjoy a relaxing evening in the park with a picnic near one of the scenic lakes or a peaceful walk along the shoreline. | Return to your lodge or campsite for the night.

DAY 3: EXPLORE JACKSON HOLE, CODY, WYOMING, BEARTOOTH HIGHWAY

7:00 AM - EXPLORE JACKSON HOLE: Start your day in Jackson Hole, Wyoming. Visit the charming town square, unique shops, art galleries, and restaurants. Admire the iconic elk antler arches.

9:00 AM - OPTIONAL ACTIVITY: Scenic Float Trip or Whitewater Rafting: If time permits, consider a scenic float trip down the Snake River or an adventurous whitewater rafting excursion.

11:30 AM - DRIVE TO CODY, WYOMING: Depart for Cody, Wyoming, located east of Yellowstone.

1:30 PM - BUFFALO BILL CENTER OF THE WEST: Visit the Buffalo Bill Center of the West, which consists of five museums dedicated to the history and culture of the American West. | Spend a couple of hours exploring the exhibits.

4:00 PM - CODY NITE RODEO (SUMMER MONTHS): If visiting during the summer, enjoy a rodeo experience at the Cody Nite Rodeo, which typically starts in the evening. | Experience the excitement of rodeo events and Western entertainment.

6:00 PM - SCENIC DRIVE ON BEARTOOTH HIGHWAY: Begin your scenic drive on the Beartooth Highway from Cody to Red Lodge, Montana.Stop at viewpoints like Rock Creek Vista Point to marvel at the stunning mountain vistas, alpine meadows, and picturesque lakes. | **8:30 PM - RETURN JOURNEY:** Take your time to return to your starting point, reflecting on the incredible experiences and natural beauty you've encountered during your trip. | **10:00 PM - END OF DAY:** Arrive back at your lodge or campground and relax after an adventurous day.

BEST 2-DAY YELLOWSTONE NATIONAL PARK ITINERARY

DAY ONE: WILDLIFE WATCHING, HOT SPRINGS, AND WATERFALLS

5:00 AM - 8:00 AM: WILDLIFE WATCHING IN LAMAR VALLEY: Head to Lamar Valley in the park's northeast corner for early morning wildlife viewing. This is your best chance to see bison, grizzly bears, elk, coyotes, wolves, moose, and bald eagles. | **TIP:** Bring binoculars or a spotting scope. Stay at least 100 yards from predators and 25 yards from other animals.

8:30 AM - 10:00 AM: MAMMOTH HOT SPRINGS: Drive to Mammoth Hot Springs near the park's north entrance. Explore the colorful travertine terraces along the 1.75-mile boardwalk. | **TIP:** The area is composed of two loops; doing both offers views of approximately 50 hot springs.

10:30 AM - 1:00 PM: HIKE TO MYSTIC FALLS: Drive to the Biscuit Basin trailhead. Hike the 2.8-mile roundtrip trail to Mystic Falls, which includes a scenic walk along the Little Firehole River and ends at a beautiful 70-foot waterfall. | **OPTIONAL EXTENSION:** Add another mile to your hike for an overlook view of the Upper Geyser Basin, home to Old Faithful.

1:30 PM - 2:30 PM: LUNCH AT OLD FAITHFUL INN: Head to the Old Faithful Inn for lunch. If you can't secure a table at the Dining Room, try the other dining options within the complex. | **TIP:** The architecture of the inn is worth exploring even if you're just stopping by for a meal.

3:00 PM - 6:00 PM: EXPLORE UPPER GEYSER BASIN: Watch Old Faithful erupt and then explore the boardwalks of Upper Geyser Basin. Walk up to 6 miles among the highest concentration of geysers in the world. | **TIP:** Check eruption predictions at _www.nps.gov/yell/planyourvisit/exploreoldfaithful.htm._

6:30 PM: CHECK-IN AND DINNER: Check into your accommodation and have dinner. If staying within the park, dining options may be available at your lodge.

DAY TWO: GEYSERS, SPRINGS, AND GRAND CANYON OF YELLOWSTONE

6:00 AM - 7:00 AM: WATCH OLD FAITHFUL ERUPT: Start your day by watching Old Faithful erupt if you didn't get a chance on Day One. | **TIP:** Early morning visits are less crowded.

7:30 AM - 9:00 AM: VISIT GRAND PRISMATIC SPRING: Head to Midway Geyser Basin to see Grand Prismatic Spring. Walk the boardwalk for up-close views or take the Fairy Falls trail for an elevated perspective. | **TIP:** The overlook on the Fairy Falls trail offers a unique vantage point.

10:00 AM - 12:00 PM: PICNIC AT YELLOWSTONE LAKE: Drive to Yellowstone Lake. Enjoy a picnic at one of the 13 designated areas, with West Thumb or Grant Village being the closest from Grand Prismatic. | **TIP:** If you didn't bring lunch, stop by Grant Village Camper Services for food.

12:30 PM - 3:30 PM: EXPLORE GRAND CANYON OF THE YELLOWSTONE: Visit the Grand Canyon of the Yellowstone. View the Upper, Lower, and Crystal Falls from various overlooks. | **Lower Falls:** Accessible from Red Rock Point, Artist Point, Lookout Point, and Brink of Lower Falls trail. | **Upper Falls:** Best seen from Brink of Upper Falls overlook. | **Crystal Falls:** Visible from the South Rim Trail.

4:00 PM: DEPARTURE: Begin your journey out of the park, reflecting on an incredible two days in Yellowstone.

3-DAY GRAND TETON ITINERARY
FOR HIKING ENTHUSIASTS

DAY ONE: CASCADE CANYON, JACKSON, HISTORIC HOMESTEADS

MORNING: HIKE CASCADE CANYON (8 MILES OUT-AND-BACK TO THE FORK)

8:00 AM - Arrive at Jenny Lake Visitor Center: Park your vehicle and prepare for the day. Use the restrooms, fill up your water bottles, and ensure you have all your hiking gear.

8:30 AM - Take the Jenny Lake Boat Shuttle: Board the boat shuttle for a 10-minute ride across Jenny Lake. The boat costs $12 one-way or $20 roundtrip. Arriving early minimizes wait times.

8:45 AM - Begin Hike to Hidden Falls and Inspiration Point: Start the hike to Hidden Falls (0.5 miles) and continue to Inspiration Point (1 mile total). This section will be crowded.

9:30 AM - Continue into Cascade Canyon: Pass Inspiration Point and head deeper into the canyon. The trail flattens out and becomes less crowded. Follow Cascade Creek, enjoying waterfalls, wildflowers, and potential wildlife sightings (moose, black bears).

12:30 PM - Reach the Fork: After approximately 4 miles, reach the fork in the trail. Decide whether to hike further to Lake Solitude or return.

1:00 PM - Return to Jenny Lake: Head back the way you came, aiming to reach the boat dock by mid-afternoon.

3:00 PM - Return Boat Shuttle: Take the boat shuttle back across Jenny Lake and return to your car.

AFTERNOON: VISIT JACKSON, WYOMING

4:00 PM - Arrive in Jackson: Drive to Jackson, a short trip from Jenny Lake.

4:30 PM - Lunch at Jackson Drug: Enjoy a creative and healthy meal to refuel after your hike.

5:30 PM - Visit Jackson Hole Historical Society and Museum: Spend an hour exploring the museum, which costs $10. Check out Native American artifacts and cowboy-era antiques.

EVENING: EXPLORE HISTORIC HOMESTEADS

7:00 PM - Visit Mormon Row Historic District: Drive back towards Grand Teton and stop at Mormon Row to see the picturesque homesteads with the Teton Range as a backdrop. Spend about 30 minutes here.

7:30 PM - Visit Menor's Ferry Historic District: Continue to Menor's Ferry to see the historic general store and the replica ferryboat. Spend about 30 minutes here.

8:00 PM - Head to Campsite: Drive to your chosen campsite. If dispersed camping, aim to arrive early to secure a spot. Set up camp and prepare for the night.

DAY TWO: TAGGART AND BRADLEY LAKES, COLTER BAY SWIM BEACH, FAMOUS VIEWPOINTS

MORNING: HIKE TAGGART AND BRADLEY LAKES (6-MILE LOOP)

7:00 AM - Arrive at Taggart Lake Trailhead: Park at the trailhead and prepare for the hike.

7:15 AM - Begin Hike: Start the loop hike, going clockwise to reach Taggart Lake first.

8:15 AM - Arrive at Taggart Lake: Enjoy the serene lake and take photos of the mountain reflections.

8:45 AM - Continue to Bradley Lake: Hike the stretch between Taggart and Bradley Lakes, being mindful of potential wildlife.

9:45 AM - Arrive at Bradley Lake: Relax by the lake, take photos, and consider a quick swim if you're up for it.

10:30 AM - Complete the Loop: Continue the hike to complete the loop back to the trailhead.

AFTERNOON: SWIM AT COLTER BAY

12:00 PM - Arrive at Colter Bay: Drive to Colter Bay Village.

12:30 PM - Lunch: If not packed, enjoy lunch at Jackson Lake Lodge's Pioneer Grill, famous for huckleberry dishes.

1:30 PM - Swim at Colter Bay Swim Beach: Spend the afternoon relaxing and swimming at the beach. Enjoy the stunning views of the Teton Range from the lake.

EVENING: VISIT SCENIC VIEWPOINTS

4:00 PM - Drive to Oxbow Bend: Take a scenic drive to Oxbow Bend, a prime spot for wildlife viewing and photography.

4:30 PM - Visit Snake River Overlook: Continue to Snake River Overlook, made famous by Ansel Adams' iconic photograph.

5:00 PM - Return to Campsite: Head back to your campsite, prepare dinner, and relax.

DAY THREE: DELTA LAKE HIKE (7.5 MILES OUT-AND-BACK)

MORNING: HIKE TO DELTA LAKE

6:30 AM - Arrive at Lupine Meadows Trailhead: Arrive early to secure parking. Use the restrooms and ensure you have plenty of water and snacks.

6:45 AM - Begin Hike: Start your ascent through switchbacks. Enjoy views of wildflower meadows and lakes from above.

8:45 AM - Begin Boulder Scramble: Navigate the boulder fields, using your hands for stability. Take your time and enjoy the challenge.

10:00 AM - Reach Delta Lake: Arrive at the stunning Delta Lake. Take in the breathtaking views of the turquoise water and the Teton Range. Relax, take photos, and consider a quick, refreshing dip.

11:30 AM - Begin Descent: Retrace your steps, descending carefully, particularly through the boulder fields.

1:30 PM - Return to Trailhead: Arrive back at the trailhead.

AFTERNOON: DEPARTURE

2:00 PM - Pack Up Camp: Return to your campsite, pack up your gear, and prepare for departure.

3:00 PM - Depart Grand Teton: Head towards your next destination, whether it's home or another adventure.

ADDITIONAL TIPS FOR YOUR GRAND TETON TRIP

Bear Safety: Always carry bear spray, make noise on the trails, and be aware of your surroundings. Store food securely at campsites.

Hydration and Nutrition: Carry plenty of water and high-energy snacks. Consider a water filtration system for longer hikes.

Weather Preparedness: Be prepared for changing weather conditions, especially at higher elevations. Pack layers and rain gear.

Leave No Trace: Follow Leave No Trace principles to preserve the natural beauty of the park for future visitors.

This itinerary offers a comprehensive and exhilarating experience for hiking enthusiasts, covering some of the most iconic and beautiful trails and sites in Grand Teton National Park. Enjoy your adventure!

CHAPTER 6: FOOD & RESTAURANTS

- Local Food to Enjoy In Yellowstone and Grand Teton
- Top Restaurants To Dine In
  - Yellowstone
  - Grand Teton
  - Jackson Hole, Wyoming
  - Cody, Wyoming

6 LOCAL FOOD TO ENJOY IN YELLOWSTONE & GRAND TETON

When visiting Yellowstone and Grand Teton National Parks, you'll have the opportunity to savor some delicious local food. Here are a few local specialties to try:

1. Bison Burger: Bison is a staple of the region and can be found on many restaurant menus. Enjoy a flavorful bison burger, which offers a unique taste compared to traditional beef burgers.

2. Huckleberries: These small, tart berries are a local favorite. You can find them in various forms, including jams, syrups, pies, and even in savory dishes like huckleberry-glazed salmon.

3. Trout: The freshwater streams and lakes in the area are home to several trout species. Enjoy a freshly caught trout dish, whether it's pan-seared, grilled, or baked.

4. Elk Steak: Elk is another game meat popular in the region. Try an elk steak for a lean and flavorful dining experience.

5. Fry Bread: Fry bread is a Native American dish that has become a staple in the region. It is a deep-fried bread with a crispy exterior and soft interior. Enjoy it on its own or topped with honey, powdered sugar, or savory ingredients like ground beef and beans.

6. Craft Beer: The Yellowstone and Grand Teton area is home to several breweries that offer a wide variety of craft beers. Sample locally brewed beers that incorporate unique flavors and ingredients inspired by the natural surroundings.

Remember to explore the surrounding towns and communities near the national parks, as they often have excellent local restaurants and eateries that serve up these regional specialties.

TOP 10 YELLOWSTONE RESTAURANTS & BARS

1. MAMMOTH GENERAL STORE

Mammoth General Store is a shop located at 315A Grand Loop Rd in Yellowstone National Park, WY. They offer fast food and grill options. The store is open everyday from 9:00am to 4:30 pm. They have a variety of items available, including souvenirs, snacks, and beverages. The store has friendly staff, good selection of gifts, and delicious ice cream. It is a convenient stop for visitors in the park.

2. THE OLD FAITHFUL BASIN STORE

The Old Faithful Basin Store in Yellowstone National Park, WY, is a convenient American diner. Open from 9 AM to 6 PM, it offers typical diner fare, including burgers and fries. Their food can sometimes be excellent and average sometimes. Their staff are friendly. The store also sells souvenirs, making it a great stop for park exploration. Facilities include takeout, seating, parking, and wheelchair accessibility. Although the website is unavailable, the menu can be found online. Overall, it serves as a practical dining option for visitors exploring the park.

3. ROOSEVELT LODGE DINING ROOM

Roosevelt Lodge Dining Room is a restaurant located at Tower-Roosevelt in Yellowstone National Park, Wyoming. They serve American cuisine and offer vegetarian-friendly and gluten-free options. You will generally enjoy your dining experience, highlighting the great location, food, and service. Recommended dishes include ribs, trout dip, burgers, and huckleberry ice cream. You might however experience long wait times and service issues.

4. OLD FAITHFUL GENERAL STORE

Old Faithful General Store is a restaurant located at 2 Old Faithful Loop Road in Yellowstone National Park, WY. They serve American cuisine and offer lunch and breakfast options. The store offers good food, reasonable prices, and convenient location near Old

Faithful. They also offer takeout services and have parking available. Vegetarian options such as salads and fruits are available on the menu. It is a popular stop for visitors in the park.

5. THE MAMMOTH HOTEL DINING ROOM

The Mammoth Hotel Dining Room in Yellowstone National Park, WY, serves delicious American cuisine. The staff is friendly and professional, and the food is praised for its excellent preparation and diverse menu. The restaurant caters to vegetarian, vegan, and gluten-free diets. However, they have limited food options due to staffing and supply challenges. Situated with a grand view of the park, the dining room offers a delightful experience for visitors exploring Yellowstone.

6. LAKE YELLOWSTONE HOTEL DINING ROOM

Lake Yellowstone Hotel Dining Room offers an elegant dining experience with upscale American cuisine and scenic views of Yellowstone Lake. The restaurant is open daily from 12:00 AM to 11:59 PM and caters to vegetarian, vegan, and gluten-free dietary preferences. You will enjoy the food and atmosphere, particularly with dishes like halibut and rainbow trout. You might however experience occasional complaints about slow service, limited food options, and high prices. The restaurant is known for its popular breakfast buffet, and reservations are recommended.

7. BEAR PIT LOUNGE

Bear Pit Lounge at Old Faithful Inn in Yellowstone National Park, WY, is an American-style bar and pub. It offers a cozy ambiance and well-mixed drinks. While the menu is limited, the draft beer and mixed drinks come highly recommended. It serves as a good option while waiting for a table in the main dining room at the Inn. Facilities include seating, parking, wheelchair accessibility, and a full bar with table service.

8. OBSIDIAN DINING ROOM

Obsidian Dining Room is an American restaurant located at 2051 Snow Lodge Ave in Yellowstone National Park, WY. They offer a menu for breakfast, lunch, and dinner, with options for vegetarians and gluten-free diets. You will particularly enjoy the bison short ribs and trout. Though you might find the menu limited and the food quality underwhelming, their Service are friendly but occasionally slow. The atmosphere is pleasant with a beautiful setting.

9. FISHING BRIDGE GENERAL STORE

Fishing Bridge General Store is a restaurant located at 1 East Entrance Road in Yellowstone National Park, WY. They serve American cuisine and offer breakfast, lunch, and dinner options. You will enjoy the good food, friendly service, and reasonable prices. The store also has a grocery section where you can find a variety of items, including meats, chicken, eggs, fresh fruits, and vegetables. It is a convenient place to stock up on groceries while visiting the park. The store offers seating, parking, wheelchair accessibility, and takeout services.

10. CANYON FOUNTAIN AND GRILL

Canyon Fountain and Grill, located at Yellowstone National Park, WY, offers American cuisine with a fast food and diner-style menu. The restaurant has U-shaped counters for a fun and friendly atmosphere with counter service. You might want to avoid their Asian cuisine. Takeout is available, and its operating hours are from 6:00 AM to 10:30 AM, 11:00 AM to 2:30 PM, and 4:30 PM to 9:30 PM.You will appreciate the convenience of grabbing a bite while exploring the park.

TOP 10 RESTAURANTS IN GRAND TETON NATIONAL PARK

1. TRAPPER GRILL

Trapper Grill at Signal Mountain Lodge offers local American cuisine, with options for vegetarians and vegans. You will enjoy the breathtaking views and convenient location. You might have mixed experiences with their food and service. It provides takeout, outdoor seating, and is wheelchair accessible. Prices are moderate to expensive, and it accepts major credit cards. Trapper Grill offers a scenic dining experience with varied food options, though with some mixed reviews.

2. LEEK'S MARINA & PIZZERIA

Leek's Marina & Pizzeria offers Italian cuisine with a focus on pizza and salads. You will enjoy the homemade quality and generous toppings of the pizza. The location provides a fantastic view of the Tetons, creating an enjoyable dining experience. You might occasionally experience burnt crust or inconsistent pizza but you will surely enjoy an overall positive experience at the restaurant. Leek's Marina & Pizzeria offers takeout, outdoor seating, parking, and is wheelchair accessible. Prices are moderate to expensive, and alcohol is served.

3. JENNY LAKE LODGE DINING ROOM

Jenny Lake Lodge Dining Room offers an expensive gourmet American cuisine experience. With a 5-course meal that rotates nightly, you will enjoy the delicious food and welcoming staff. The atmosphere is rustic and elegant, offering scenic mountain views. This restaurant is highly recommended for special occasions. It provides facilities like reservations, seating, free off-street parking, and is wheelchair accessible. Jenny Lake Lodge Dining Room offers a delightful dining experience amid the natural beauty of the park.

4. THE MURAL ROOM

The Mural Room serves American cuisine with vegetarian-friendly and vegan options. Operating daily from 7:00 AM to 9:30 AM, 11:30 AM to 1:30 PM, and 5:30 PM to 9:00 PM, the restaurant offers a splendid view of the Tetons through floor-to-ceiling windows. You will appreciate the historic decor and ambiance with excellent meals and services. You might however encountered inconsistencies in food quality and slow service. Prices range from $20 to $50.

5. PIZZA PASTA CO @ DORNANS

Pizza Pasta Co @ Dornans offers Italian and American cuisine, including a variety of pizzas and pasta dishes. Their delicious pizza is highly recommend and you will enjoy the restaurant's scenic views and atmosphere, providing an excellent spot to enjoy the Teton Range. It is a must-visit place where you can experience occasional service issues due to crowds. With moderate to expensive prices, Pizza Pasta Co @ Dornans offers a delightful dining experience in a picturesque setting.

6. PIONEER GRILL AT JACKSON LAKE LODGE

Pioneer Grill at Jackson Lake Lodge offers American diner cuisine with a retro atmosphere. The restaurant operates from 6:00 AM to 10:00 PM, serving menu items such as burgers, sandwiches, pancakes, and salads, with prices ranging from $8 to $20. You will appreciate the friendly service and tasty, fresh food. Though you might experience occasional service issues, Pioneer Grill is generally considered a good choice for a quick meal while visiting Jackson Lake Lodge. Gluten-free options are available if you are with dietary preferences.

7. THE BLUE HERON

The Blue Heron offers American cuisine and serves as a bar. You will enjoy the breathtaking views of Jackson Lake and the Tetons from the restaurant. The food and drinks are generally considered decent. The menu includes options like burgers, soups, sandwiches, and drinks, with prices ranging from $5 to $23. The restaurant provides vegetarian-friendly options with operating hours varying.

The overall experience is highly recommended, especially for the view.

8. THE RANCH HOUSE AT COLTER BAY

The Ranch House at Colter Bay offers American cuisine with vegetarian-friendly options. Prices range from $8 to $28. You will enjoy the good food and service, including vegetarian dishes and friendly staff. You might however encountered issues like small portions, limited choices, and inconsistent quality.

9. SHEFFIELDS RESTAURANT & SALOON

Sheffields Restaurant & Saloon offers American cuisine with specialties like trout and elk. The restaurant has a rustic atmosphere that complements the national park setting. You will enjoy the delicious food and friendly service. While the menu is not extensive, the dishes are well-prepared. You might however experience longer wait times and occasional mediocre food experiences. The restaurant provides seating, parking (free off-street), highchairs, and is wheelchair accessible. It serves alcohol, including wine and beer.

10. DEADMAN'S BAR

Deadman's Bar serves American cuisine as a bar and pub. Operating from 7:00 AM to 12:00 AM, it offers breakfast, lunch, and dinner. The restaurant features seating, parking, television, and is wheelchair accessible. You will appreciate the convenience of the bar while staying in the park. The food and drinks are generally praised, with nachos being a standout item. The friendly service and relaxed atmosphere make it a great spot to unwind after exploring the park.

TOP 5 RESTAURANTS IN
JACKSON HOLE, WYOMING

1. THE BLUE LION

The Blue Lion is a restaurant located at 160 N Millward St, Jackson, WY 83001-8580. They can be contacted at +1 307-733-3912. The restaurant offers American, Seafood, and International cuisine. Operating hours are from 5:30 pm to 9:00 pm, Wednesday to Monday. The menu features dishes such as rack of lamb, elk, fresh fish, lobster and shrimp scampi, beef tenderloin, Marsala Florentine with chicken, and vegetarian options. The price range for food is between $22 and $48. The restaurant provides facilities such as takeout, parking, highchairs, reservations, outdoor seating, a full bar, live music, and gift cards. You will enjoy the food quality and service at The Blue Lion with dishes like elk tenderloin, bison short ribs, crab-stuffed mushrooms, gnocchi, scallops.

2. LOCAL RESTAURANT & BAR

Local Restaurant & Bar, located at 55 N Cache St, Jackson, WY 83001-8680, offers American cuisine in a bar setting. They serve lunch, dinner, and late-night meals. The menu features a diverse range of options, including steak, charcuterie, oysters, trout, wedge salad, brussel sprouts, elk chop, pork, and more. Prices range from $30 to $50 per dish. The restaurant provides facilities such as reservations, seating, television, highchairs, wheelchair accessibility, and a full bar. You will the great cocktails and food, particularly the steak, fries, fried macaroni, crab cake, shrimp cocktail, and mac & cheese bites. You might however experience minor issues with reservations or specific dishes, but overall, Local Restaurant & Bar is highly recommended for a pleasant dining experience.

3. MIAZGA'S

Miazga's, located at 399 W Broadway Ave, Jackson, WY 83001-8637, is an Italian and Polish restaurant. The menu offers dishes such as kielbasa, cannoli, meatball subs, spaghetti, lobster rolls, Reubens, spinach dip, berry pie, and more. The price range for food is $10 - $18. The restaurant provides facilities like vegetarian-friendly options and vegan options. You will enjoy the fresh food, outstanding service, and delicious Polish comfort food.

4. TRIO AN AMERICAN BISTRO

Trio An American Bistro, located at 45 S Glenwood St, Jackson, WY 83001-8759, is an upscale American restaurant. The menu offers a variety of dishes including risotto, pizza, pork chops, salad, bread, half chicken, and more. The price range for food is $30. The restaurant provides facilities like vegetarian-friendly options, vegan options, and gluten-free options. You will enjoy the remarkable dining experience, great food, and top-notch service. Though you might encounter unattentive service provision or minor issues, it is however recommended as a special place for a meal.

5. SNAKE RIVER GRILL

Snake River Grill, located at 84 E Broadway Ave, Jackson, WY 83001-8630, is an American restaurant known for its fine dining experience. The menu features mostly organic and seasonal foods, fresh seafood, prime chops and steaks, vegetarian dishes, and free-range game and chicken. The restaurant has been nominated by the James Beard Foundation for "Best Chef North West" and has received Wine Spectator's "Award of Excellence" for its extensive wine selection. You will particularly enjoy the food, service, and atmosphere of the restaurant. Specific dishes like the pork shank, onion rings, potato pancakes, steak, are highly recommended.

TOP 5 RESTAURANTS IN
CODY, WYOMING

1. OUR PLACE CAFÉ

Our Place Café is a local restaurant located at 148 Yellowstone Ave, Cody, WY. It offers American and local cuisine in a cafe and diner setting. The restaurant provides breakfast, lunch, and brunch menus. Its current operating hours are 6:00am to 1:00pm on Sundays, Wednesdays, Thursdays, Fridays and Saturdays. You will enjoy the food, especially the breakfast options with their friendly staff and pleasant atmosphere. While the restaurant can get busy, the wait will be a worthwhile one. it is an highly recommended restaurant particularly for breakfast.

2. PAT'S BREW HOUSE

Pat's Brew House is a local restaurant and brew pub situated at 1019 15th St, Cody, WY. They offer American and local cuisine, along with a variety of beers brewed on-site. The restaurant's operating hours are 11:00am to 9:00pm Sunday, Wednesday, Thursday, Friday, Saturday. Their menu includes lunch, dinner, and drinks, with food prices ranging from $12 to $22. Pat's Brew House provides several facilities, such as free Wifi, takeout, outdoor seating, parking, televisions, wheelchair accessibility, and a full bar serving alcohol. They also offer live music and are dog-friendly in a non-smoking environment. You will enjoy the locally brewed beer and tasty pub fare, along with the relaxing atmosphere and friendly staff. Though the place can get busy, the service is generally quick. Pat's Brew House is a great spot to enjoy good food and drinks.

3. BUBBA'S BAR-B-QUE

Bubba's Bar-B-Que in Cody, Wyoming, offers American cuisine with gluten-free options for breakfast, lunch, and dinner. Their menu boasts favorites like sausage and bacon burritos, biscuits and gravy, French toast, omelettes, BBQ pork, chicken, ribs, and brisket. The restaurant operates from 7:00 AM to 9:00 PM, serving moderately priced dishes. Amenities include seating, a salad bar (availability varies), and takeout. You will enjoy the delicious brisket, BBQ sauce, and generous portions. It's a popular spot known for tasty BBQ and friendly service.

4. CODY STEAKHOUSE

Cody Steakhouse in Cody, WY, offers American cuisine, specializing in steaks and a full bar. The restaurant's operating hours are 4:00pm to 9:00pm Monday to Saturday. The menu is available on their website: _https://codysteakhouse.com,_ featuring dishes ranging from $9 to $42. Facilities include reservations, seating, highchairs, a full bar, credit card acceptance, and gift cards availability. You will enjoy the delicious food, prompt service, and friendly staff. The steaks, drinks, sides, and desserts along with the extensive wine list will give you an overall positive dining experience. You might however experience unpleasant staff attitude or feeling rushed during the meal.

5. 8TH STREET AT THE IVY

8th Street at the Ivy is an American cuisine restaurant located at 1800 8th St, Cody, WY. They offer breakfast and lunch from 7:00 AM to 2:00 PM and dinner from 5:00 PM to 9:00 PM. The food prices range from $7 to $34, and the menu is available on their website _https://8thstreetattheivy.com_ . The restaurant caters to various dietary preferences, providing vegetarian-friendly, vegan, and gluten-free options. You will enjoy the excellent food, generous portions, well-cooked dishes, and friendly staff. Recommended dishes include pancakes, meatloaf, spaghetti, and the Reuben sandwich. You might however experience service issues or dry meatloaf.

YOUR FEEDBACK

Thank You So Much For Reading this Far!

I sincerely appreciate the time you've taken to read my book this far. As a small independent publisher, your support means a great deal, and I hope my guide is making a difference in your traveling journey. If you could spare just 60 seconds, I would love to hear your honest feedback on Amazon. Your reviews are incredibly valuable and help other travelers too. To leave your feedback, follow the steps below:

1. Open your camera app | 2. Scan the QR code below with your mobile device | 3. The review page will open in your web browser | 4. Write your review and submit.

OR ENTER THE URL BELOW IN YOUR BROWSER

https://tinyurl.com/yellgtnp

When the review page opens, Rate this guide with stars (one to five) based on your experience from reading/using this guide. | Write a review in the provided text box. | Proofread and submit. | Allow a few days for your review to appear.

Thank you so much!

CHAPTER 7: WHERE TO STAY IN YELLOWSTONE AND GRAND TETON

- 10 Budget-Friendly Places to Stay In Yellowstone
- 7 Budget-Friendly Places To Stay In Grand Teton National Park
- Best Campground To Stay In Grand Teton National Park

10 BUDGET-FRIENDLY PLACES TO STAY IN YELLOWSTONE NATIONAL PARK

1. PINE EDGE CABINS

Pine Edge Cabins, situated just one mile from Yellowstone National Park's North East Gate in Silver Gate, Montana, offers seven comfortable cabins starting from $220 to $295 per night (excluding cleaning and tax). You can enjoy a serene natural setting with scenic mountain views and the possibility of spotting wildlife like mountain goats, elk, and bison. The town of Silver Gate, founded in 1932 with a unique log and rustic architecture, adds to the charm. With its proximity to Yellowstone and the abundance of wildlife, Pine Edge Cabins provides an ideal retreat for travelers seeking a peaceful Montana experience.

2. ABSAROKA LODGE

Yellowstone's Absaroka Lodge in Gardiner, Montana, offers a beautiful location overlooking the Yellowstone River and is just two blocks from the historic Roosevelt Arch entrance to Yellowstone National Park. The lodge provides clean and updated rooms, some with private balconies. You can enjoy the views of wildlife and the river from the balconies. Amenities include free Wi-Fi, coffee makers, and microwaves. While there may be occasional Wi-Fi issues, you will appreciated the lodging's proximity to the park and the clean accommodations. Prices range from $227 to $274 for a standard room.

3. GRANT VILLAGE LODGE

Grant Village Lodge is located near the West Thumb of Yellowstone Lake, offering 300 non-smoking rooms and family accommodations. The lodge features basic amenities, including free parking, a restaurant, and a convenience store. Although the rooms are clean, you might find them small and outdated, lacking modern comforts like Wi-Fi and TVs. The picturesque location provides easy access to Yellowstone's attractions, making it a suitable choice if you seek a convenient stay within the park. Prices ranges from $293 to $413 per night. some visitors feel it's overpriced for the level of comfort provided.

4. ROOSEVELT LODGE CABINS

Roosevelt Lodge Cabins, located near Yellowstone's Tower Falls area, offers a rustic and charming experience in the heart of nature. The cabins, dating back to 1920, provide a cozy retreat for families and fishermen alike. Situated close to a campsite once used by President Theodore Roosevelt, the lodge's front porch rocking chairs allow guests to relax and embrace their "Old West spirit." The extensive corral operation provides horseback trail rides and stagecoach adventures, while the well-liked Old West Dinner Cookout presents visitors with delicious steaks, friendly wranglers, and awe-inspiring landscapes. The lodge is an ideal spot to immerse yourself in Yellowstone's serene beauty and wildlife.

5. LAKE YELLOWSTONE HOTEL AND COTTAGES

Lake Yellowstone Hotel and Cottages, located in Yellowstone National Park, offers various room types with amenities such as views of Yellowstone Lake, comfortable beds, and private bathrooms. Nearby attractions include Storm Point Trail and Bridge Bay Marina. The hotel features an on-site restaurant, lounge, free parking, and a gift shop. Additionally, there is a business center equipped with internet connectivity. The average nightly price is $359 and above, with prices varying based on room type and date. The historic hotel provides a classic yet casual elegance, making it an ideal choice for those seeking a charming stay in the park.

6. OLD FAITHFUL INN

Old Faithful Inn is an iconic lodge in Yellowstone National Park, WY, is located close to the famous Old Faithful geyser, offering beautiful views. The inn was built in 1903-1904 and is considered the largest log structure globally. It has 327 rooms, including options with a geyser view. Amenities include a restaurant, lounge, and free parking. However, there is no AC, TV, or WiFi in the rooms. Prices range from $558 to $649 per night. You'll appreciate the historic charm and proximity to geysers.

7. OLD FAITHFUL LODGE CABINS

Old Faithful Lodge Cabins in Yellowstone National Park offers 96 cabins with basic amenities like one or two double beds, a sink, and a private bathroom. The cabins do not have televisions or air conditioning. The location is excellent, close to attractions like Old Faithful Geyser, Upper Geyser Basin, and Grand Prismatic Spring. The lodge provides free parking, an on-site restaurant, and opportunities for hiking and picnicking. The rooms are small but clean, making it a suitable option for travelers who prioritize location and natural surroundings over luxurious accommodations.

8. MAMMOTH HOT SPRINGS HOTEL & CABINS

Mammoth Hot Springs Hotel & Cabins is located at 2 Mammoth Hotel Avenue, Mammoth, WY 82190. The hotel offers 257 rooms, including cabins with various amenities such as a sink, coffee maker, and fridge. You can enjoy an on-site restaurant and lounge, as well as free parking. The hotel is situated close to popular attractions like Yellowstone National Park and Mammoth Hot Springs. It offers wheelchair access and has mountain views. The price range for rooms at Mammoth Hot Springs Hotel & Cabins varies depending on the room type, season, and availability. On average, prices can range from $171 to $444 per night for a standard room.

9. CANYON LODGE AND CABINS

Canyon Lodge and Cabins is a well-located hotel in Yellowstone National Park, offering 520 rooms and cabins. The property features an on-site restaurant, free parking, and paid internet access. Nearby attractions include Grand Canyon of the Yellowstone, Lower Yellowstone River Falls, and Artist Point. Room amenities include a refrigerator, coffee maker, and non-smoking rooms. Prices range from $364 to $589 for a standard room. The lodge is known for its convenient location and clean, comfortable accommodations, making it a popular choice for visitors exploring the park's natural wonders.

10. LAKE LODGE CABINS

Lake Lodge Cabins in Yellowstone National Park offer 186 cabins in three styles: Western, Frontier, and Pioneer. The cabins feature private bathrooms, heating, and basic amenities like a coffee pot and refrigerator. However, there is no Wi-Fi or TV available. The property provides free parking and has an on-site restaurant and lounge. Nearby attractions include Storm Point Trail and Bridge Bay Marina. While the exterior may look outdated, the cabins are modern and comfortable inside. The average rate for a standard room ranges from $281 to $366. It's a great place to stay for nature enthusiasts seeking a serene experience.

7 BUDGET-FRIIENDLY PLACES TO STAY
IN GRAND TETON NATIONAL PARK

1. JACKSON LAKE LODGE

Jackson Lake Lodge is a full-service resort hotel located in Grand Teton National Park, Wyoming. It offers breathtaking views of the Teton Range and Jackson Lake. The lodge provides various amenities like free parking, pool, bar/lounge, and activities for families. The rooms have private balconies, safes, and irons, though no TVs. It houses several dining options and a scenic lobby with floor-to-ceiling windows. The lodge is well-located for exploring nearby attractions like Jackson Lake and Signal Mountain Summit Road. Prices range from $384 to $512 per night.

2. COLTER BAY VILLAGE

Colter Bay Village is a charming accommodation in Grand Teton National Park, Wyoming. It offers rustic cabins with comfortable beds and modern bathrooms, but no TV, Wi-Fi, hairdryer, fridge, or microwave. The property features an on-site restaurant, free parking, and kids' activities. Nearby attractions include Jackson Lake, Chapel of the Sacred Heart, and Hermitage Point. The village provides a peaceful and quiet environment, ideal for exploring the national park. With 209 cabins available, the average nightly rate ranges from $380 to $381 for a standard room. It offers a unique and affordable vacation experience amidst the stunning natural surroundings.

3. JENNY LAKE LODGE

Jenny Lake Lodge, located in Grand Teton National Park, offers elegant cabins with stunning mountain views. The lodge provides a luxurious and peaceful experience amidst nature's beauty. It is open seasonally from June to early October and offers gourmet breakfast and nightly five-course dinner as part of its Signature Stay package. You can enjoy various activities, such as horseback riding and cycling, while exploring nearby attractions like Jenny Lake and Cascade Canyon Trail. With 37 rooms available, the lodge provides modern amenities like free WiFi, complimentary toiletries & housekeeping. Prices range from $1,149 to $1,227 per night for a standard room.

4. HEADWATERS LODGE & CABINS AT FLAGG RANCH

Headwaters Lodge & Cabins at Flagg Ranch is located in **Moran, Wyoming,** close to Grand Teton National Park and Yellowstone National Park. It offers cabins, RV sites, tent sites, and camper cabins. The lodge provides amenities like free parking, a coffee shop, hiking, horseback riding, and pet-friendly accommodations. There are 92 rooms available with features such as housekeeping and refrigerators. Nearby attractions include John D Rockefeller Jr Memorial Parkway, Moose Falls, and Snake River. Prices range from $289 to $382 per night for a standard room. The lodge provides a peaceful and convenient base for exploring the surrounding national parks.

5. SIGNAL MOUNTAIN LODGE

Signal Mountain Lodge is a resort in Grand Teton National Park, Wyoming. It offers 79 rooms in stand-alone cabins with private balconies and scenic views. The lodge provides a variety of amenities, including three restaurants, a bar, a convenience store, and gift shops. You can enjoy activities such as canoeing, hiking, guided fishing, and scenic Snake River float trips. The location is central to many attractions, including Jackson Lake and Chapel of the Sacred Heart. While you will enjoy the lodge's ambiance and views, you might experience issues with bed comfort and limited amenities.

6. TRIANGLE X RANCH

Triangle X Ranch is a highly-rated specialty lodging located in Moose, Wyoming, within the Grand Teton National Park. The ranch offers excellent views and a range of activities like horseback riding and river floats. You will enjoy their professional and courteous staff, well-trained horses, and delicious dining options. The scenic float trips on the Snake River offer opportunities to spot wildlife like bald eagles and moose. The ranch provides non-smoking rooms and family accommodations with mountain views. With only six rooms available, it ensures an intimate & personalized experience. Free parking & airport transportation are also provided.

7. THE GRAND TETON CLIMBERS' RANCH

The Grand Teton Climbers' Ranch in Grand Teton National Park offers hostel-style accommodations for climbers and mountaineers. Located along the inner park road, it provides dormitory-style lodging in small log cabins for four to eight people. Amenities include a cook shelter, communal toilets, and hot showers (bring your own bedding and towels). Reservations are necessary, and rates are approximately $16 for AAC members and $25 for non-members. The ranch has a historic background, previously operating as the Double Diamond Ranch from 1924 to the late 1960s before the American Alpine Club established the Climbers' Ranch in 1970. To book a reservation at the Grand Teton Climbers' Ranch, you can either do it online https://americanalpineclub.org or call 307-733-7271. Reservations are necessary to secure your accommodation. Additionally, during their spring Work Week, the ranch offers free accommodations to volunteers. For more information about this opportunity, feel free to contact them through the provided phone number.

BEST CAMPGROUND TO STAY
IN GRAND TETON

1. Colter Bay Campground, located in Colter Bay Village, operates from late May to late September. It offers 324 standard sites, 13 electric hookup sites, ten hiker/biker sites, and ten group sites. Amenities include pay showers, laundry, and dump stations, with RVs up to 45 feet allowed. | *2. The Colter Bay RV Park*, situated within Colter Bay Village, is available for visitors from the beginning of May until early October. It has 102 pull-through sites and ten back-in sites, with no RV length restrictions. Amenities include pay showers and laundry. | *3. Gros Ventre Campground*, near Mormon Row Historic District, is available from late April to mid-October. The campground offers 279 regular sites, 39 sites with electric hookups, and 4 group sites. RVs up to 45 feet are allowed, with a dump station available. | *4. Jenny Lake Campground*, located near Jenny Lake and Cascade Canyon, operates from early May to late September. The park provides 51 regular sites and ten sites specifically designated for hikers and bikers. This campground is tent-only, and campers can access pay showers. | *5. Signal Mountain Campground*, close to Signal Mountain Summit Road, opens from mid-May to mid-October. It features 56 standard sites and 25 sites with electric hookups. Amenities include pay showers, laundry, and a dump station, with RVs up to 30 feet allowed. | *6. Lizard Creek Campground*, situated along John D. Rockefeller Jr. Memorial Highway, is available from mid-June to mid-September. It offers 60 standard campsites, accommodating RVs up to 30 feet in length. | *7. Headwaters Campground*, located near the Flagg Ranch Information Station, it operates from mid-May through September & offers 34 standard sites, 96 pull-through sites with full hookups, and 40 camper cabins. Campers have access to shower facilities, and the sites can accommodate RVs up to 45 feet in length.

CHAPTER 8: GETTING AROUND
YELLOWSTONE & GRAND TETON
NATIONAL PARKS

When visiting Yellowstone and Grand Teton National Parks, there are several transportation options to consider for getting around the parks and exploring the surrounding areas. Here are some transportation options you should consider:

PRIVATE VEHICLE

The most common and convenient way to explore the parks is by private vehicle. Both Yellowstone and Grand Teton have well-maintained roads that allow access to major attractions and viewpoints. Having a private vehicle gives you the freedom to create your own itinerary and explore at your own pace. However, it's important to note that parking can be limited at popular attractions, and traffic can be congested during peak seasons.

SHUTTLE SERVICES

Both Yellowstone and Grand Teton offer shuttle services within the parks. These shuttle services are operated by authorized providers and offer transportation to popular destinations and trailheads. They can be a convenient option if you prefer not to drive or want to reduce your environmental impact. Check with the respective park websites for shuttle schedules and routes.

GUIDED TOURS

Joining a guided tour is another option for exploring the parks. There are various tour companies that offer guided tours of Yellowstone and Grand Teton, providing transportation, knowledgeable guides, and planned itineraries. This option is suitable if you prefer a more structured experience and want to learn about the parks' natural and cultural history from a knowledgeable guide.

BICYCLES

Bicycles are allowed on most roads and designated bike paths within the parks. Renting a bicycle can be a great way to explore the parks at a leisurely pace, enjoying the scenic beauty and avoiding traffic congestion. Some areas, such as the Old Faithful and Mammoth Hot Springs, have bike rental facilities.

HIKING

Both Yellowstone and Grand Teton have extensive networks of hiking trails that allow you to explore on foot. Hiking is a fantastic way to immerse yourself in the parks' natural beauty and experience the serenity of the wilderness. However, it's important to be prepared, follow safety guidelines, and carry proper equipment when embarking on hikes.

PUBLIC TRANSPORTATION

Outside of the parks, public transportation options are available in nearby towns like Jackson, Cody, and West Yellowstone. These options include buses, shuttles, and taxis. Public transportation can be useful for getting to and from the parks, as well as for exploring the surrounding areas without a private vehicle.

GETTING AROUND YELLOWSTONE

The most efficient way to travel within Yellowstone National Park is by car, as there is no public transportation. Car rentals are available at nearby airports, including Yellowstone Regional (COD) in Cody, Jackson Hole (JAC) in Jackson, Yellowstone (WYS) in West Yellowstone, and Bozeman Yellowstone International (BZN) in Bozeman. *While parking is available throughout the park,* it might be difficult to find a spot depending on the season and time of day. Additionally, guided tours of the park can be arranged for those who prefer guided exploration. For visiting various regions and attractions within Yellowstone, a car is essential. The park boasts 310 miles of paved roads, making navigation relatively straightforward. However, it's important to note that road closures may occur due to snowfall and construction, so it's advisable to check the National Park Service website for advisories before embarking on your journey. Additionally, gas stations are limited within Yellowstone, and GPS devices might not always provide accurate directions. Hence, it is recommended to use an official Yellowstone map (accessible online or at the park's five visitor centers) or rely on specific GPS coordinates provided by the NPS for Yellowstone visitors. Numerous reputable companies provide guided bus and van tours within the park. These tours originate from visitor areas within Yellowstone and gateway communities such as West Yellowstone, Gardiner, and Jackson, among others. The tour fees differ depending on the company, and their operating dates also vary.

| **Useful Websites:** *https://www.budget.com* | *https://www.avis.com* | *https://www.enterprise.com* | *https://www.hertz.com/rentacar/reservation* | *https://www.yellowstonevacations.com/guided-tours* | *http://www.jacksonholealltrans.com* | *https://seeyellowstone.com*

YELLOWSTONE SNOWCOACH
TRANSPORTATION

During winter in Yellowstone, access to the interior is limited to snowcoaches, the modern heated equivalent of sleighs, traveling on groomed snow-covered roads used in summer. Experienced drivers lead guided tours, showcasing the park's extraordinary winter scenery. Snowcoach transportation to and from Old Faithful Snow Lodge is essential, available daily between Mammoth and Old Faithful Snow Lodge, with reservations possible online or by phone. Pets, except service dogs, are prohibited on snowcoaches due to federal law. Dressing in layers and wearing appropriate footwear is crucial, as stops expose passengers to varied weather conditions. Limited space allows two pieces of luggage, a small carry-on, and either cross-country skis or snowshoes. Securely closing and using durable materials for luggage is recommended. Children under three travel free, check-in is 15 minutes before departure, and regular snowcoach service from the South entrance can be arranged with Scenic Safaris.

GETTING AROUND GRAND TETON

Exploring Grand Teton National Park is best done by car, offering flexibility to discover the park at your own pace. For a $35 entrance fee, your vehicle and its occupants can access the park for seven days. Due to the park's vast size, exploring solely on foot is impractical. Many travelers fly into Jackson Hole Airport (JAC), located 5 miles from the park's Jackson entrance, or opt for Idaho Falls Regional Airport (IDA), 90 miles west, or Salt Lake City International Airport (SLC) for potentially cheaper rates. From Salt Lake City, you can rent a car for the five-hour drive to the park, while others use shuttle services like Jackson Hole Alltrans (*https://www.jacksonholealltrans.com*) or Salt Lake Express (*https://saltlakeexpress.com*).

BY CAR: Rental cars can be obtained at the airports in Jackson Hole, Idaho Falls, and Salt Lake City. While driving within the park, it's crucial to be cautious, as many of the roads are narrow two-lane routes. Adhering to the posted speed limits is especially important on popular roads like U.S. Highway 26/81/191, which links Jackson Lake to Jackson Hole, as speeding has resulted in accidents involving wildlife. The maximum speed allowed during nighttime is 45 mph. Upon entering the park, motorists are required to pay the $35 per vehicle entrance fee, which grants a seven-day permit for park access. If visiting during winter, renting an all-wheel-drive vehicle is advisable to ensure safer navigation on snowy roads. To avoid crowded parking lots, plan to visit the park before 9 a.m. or after 4 p.m.

ON FOOT: While it's recommended to explore some of the park's trails on foot, Grand Teton's vast expanse of 485 square miles makes solely relying on walking impractical. Use your car to reach chosen trailheads, and then enjoy the various miles of hiking trails within the park.

CHAPTER 9: NIGHTLIFE, FESIVALS AND EVENTS

- Nightlife in Yellowstone and Grand Teton
- Festivals in Yellowstone and Grand Teton
- Events in Yellowstone and Grand Teton

NIGHTLIFE IN YELLOWSTONE
& GRAND TETON

Yellowstone and Grand Teton National Parks are primarily known for their natural beauty and outdoor activities, so the nightlife in the parks is relatively subdued. However, there are still opportunities to enjoy evenings in the area. Here are a few options:

EVENING WILDLIFE WATCHING: Many animals are active during the early morning and evening hours, making sunset and twilight a prime time for wildlife viewing. Join a ranger-led program or venture out on your own to observe wildlife like elk, moose, and bison as they graze in the meadows or near water sources.

STAR GAZING: Due to their remote locations and limited light pollution, Yellowstone and Grand Teton offer excellent conditions for stargazing. On clear nights, you can marvel at the vast expanse of stars and maybe even catch a glimpse of the Milky Way. Look for designated stargazing programs or find a quiet spot away from artificial lights to enjoy the celestial display.

CAMPFIRE ACTIVITIES: If you're camping in the parks or staying at a lodge with campfire facilities, you can unwind around a campfire. Share stories, roast marshmallows, and enjoy the company of fellow travelers or friends and family.

EDUCATIONAL PROGRAMS AND EVENING TALKS: Check the park's visitor centers for evening educational programs and talks hosted by rangers and experts. These programs cover a range of topics, including wildlife, geology, and park history. They provide an opportunity to learn and gain a deeper understanding of the parks' natural and cultural significance.

FESTIVALS IN YELLOWSTONE
& GRAND TETON

1. YELLOWSTONE HARVEST FESTIVAL

The festival offers an impressive lineup of country and bluegrass artists like The Steeldrivers and The Grascals, guaranteeing exceptional live music. Besides, there are over 50 arts and crafts vendors offering handcrafted items, and various food trucks with local Montana cuisine. The event caters to all ages, with family-friendly activities such as face painting, games, and a petting zoo. Additionally, the festival's location near the Yellowstone River provides opportunities for outdoor enthusiasts to enjoy fishing, hiking, and kayaking, embracing Montana's natural beauty. Attendees can enjoy a vibrant atmosphere filled with music, arts, delicious food, and exciting outdoor activities throughout the event.

2. YELLOWSTONE SKI FESTIVAL

The Yellowstone Ski Festival in West Yellowstone, Montana, is a beloved Thanksgiving tradition celebrating Nordic skiing. Held in late November or early December, the festival features cross-country skiing on groomed trails, with races, clinics, and demos for all skill levels. The Rendezvous Ski Trails offer over 50 kilometers of meticulously groomed paths. An indoor expo showcases top-notch ski gear for enthusiasts to upgrade their equipment. The event also includes presentations by esteemed Nordic skiers & Olympiads. Families can enjoy a kids' zone, snowshoe hikes, and bonfire gatherings. Beyond skiing, participants can immerse themselves in Montana's scenic wilderness & foster connections with fellow skiers. The festival offers a memorable, festive experience that skiing enthusiasts shouldn't miss.

3. YELLOWSTONE INTERNATIONAL ARTS FESTIVAL

The Yellowstone International Arts Festival in Gardiner, Montana, near Yellowstone National Park, showcases classical performing arts with global artists. Founded in 2019 by the MacKay family, the festival includes dancers, musicians, and more. Produced by Youth Arts in Action, the nonprofit emphasizes arts education for youth. Usually held in late July or early August, past performers hail from prestigious companies like the Paris Opera Ballet and San Francisco Ballet. Educational workshops and outreach programs for local youth complement the performances. The festival offers a cultural experience amidst Montana's breathtaking scenery, making it a must-visit for those exploring Yellowstone National Park during that time. Enjoy world-class performances, workshops, and family-friendly activities at this captivating event.

4. MOUNTAIN MAN RENDEZVOUS

The Mountain Man Rendezvous in Cody, Wyoming, near Yellowstone National Park, is a living history event that reenacts the 1800s fur trade era. It offers muzzleloading rifle competitions, buckskinning, black powder demonstrations, and Native American skills. The rendezvous recreates the historic gatherings where mountain men traded furs, socialized, and shared knowledge. Modern visitors can experience this era firsthand, learning about fur trade history and meeting passionate living history enthusiasts. Held in July or August, the rendezvous provides an opportunity to witness rifle competitions, learn fur trade skills, and enjoy Native American demonstrations. The trade fair offers authentic fur trade-era goods, and visitors can revel in music and dancing. Embrace the Wyoming wilderness and history at this fascinating event.

5. GRAND TETON MUSIC FESTIVAL

The annual Grand Teton Music Festival in Jackson Hole, Wyoming, established in 1962, has become one of the largest and most prestigious classical music events in the United States. It offers diverse classical music performances, ranging from chamber music to orchestral concerts. Held at Walk Festival Hall in Teton Village, situated in the heart of Grand Teton National Park, the festival provides a scenic and captivating setting. Moreover, attendees can engage in educational programs like master classes, lectures, and children's concerts, alongside outreach initiatives such as free community concerts and scholarships for young musicians. The family-friendly atmosphere makes it an ideal destination for classical music enthusiasts worldwide. Experience the enchanting world of classical music amidst the beauty of Grand Teton National Park by attending this remarkable festival during your visit to Jackson Hole.

6. FIRE IN THE MOUNTAINS FESTIVAL

The Fire in the Mountains Festival is a popular music and camping event located in Moran, Wyoming, just outside Grand Teton National Park. Founded in 2008 by musicians aiming to celebrate the beauty of the Teton Mountains and the power of music, the festival has grown to become a regional favorite. Held over three days in late June or early July, it features diverse performances in bluegrass, folk, and country genres, attracting both up-and-coming and established artists. Attendees can enjoy camping on a picturesque campground, participate in outdoor activities like hiking, biking, and fishing, and attend engaging workshops and seminars on various topics. This family-friendly festival offers an opportunity to bask in the allure of the Teton Mountains, revel in outstanding music, and create cherished memories with loved ones. Plan your visit to the area to experience the magic of the Fire in the Mountains Festival.

7. TETON RAPTOR RENDEZVOUS

The Teton Raptor Rendezvous is an annual educational event held in Jackson Hole, Wyoming, dedicated to raising awareness about raptors, or birds of prey. Taking place in March or April during the raptor migration period, the event offers a unique opportunity to observe these magnificent birds up close and learn about their significance to the ecosystem. Organized by the non-profit Teton Raptor Center, known for rehabilitating and releasing raptors, the rendezvous features informative programs on raptor biology, behavior, and conservation. Attendees can also enjoy captivating live bird shows showcasing the remarkable abilities of these birds.

Families will find a welcoming and relaxed atmosphere, with engaging activities for children. Meet the experts from the Teton Raptor Center and gain valuable insights into their vital conservation work. For those interested in understanding and appreciating raptors, the Teton Raptor Rendezvous is a must-attend event while in the Jackson Hole area during the designated period.

8. JACKSON HOLE FALL ARTS FESTIVAL

The Jackson Hole Fall Arts Festival is an annual event in Wyoming's Jackson Hole, held over 12 days in September. It features diverse art exhibitions, including paintings, sculptures, and photography, alongside live music in bluegrass, jazz, and rock genres. The festival showcases local and national artists, such as Dennis Ziemienski, Ewoud De Groot, and Kathryn Mapes Turner. Visitors can also enjoy a variety of culinary delights from numerous food and drink vendors. This family-friendly festival offers activities for children in a relaxed and welcoming atmosphere, all set against the backdrop of the Teton Mountains.

EVENTS IN YELLOWSTONE
& GRAND TETON

1. RANGER PROGRAMS AND INTERPRETIVE TALKS: Throughout the year, both parks offer a range of ranger-led programs and interpretive talks. These events cover topics such as geology, wildlife, and cultural history. Check with the park's visitor centers for the latest schedule and details.

2. ART EXHIBITIONS AND WORKSHOPS: Occasionally, art exhibitions and workshops are held in the parks, showcasing the work of local and visiting artists. These events provide an opportunity to appreciate nature-inspired artwork and learn from talented artists.

3. PHOTOGRAPHY WORKSHOPS: Both Yellowstone and Grand Teton offer photography workshops led by professional photographers. These workshops focus on capturing the beauty of the parks' landscapes and wildlife. Participants can learn valuable techniques and tips while exploring scenic locations.

It's important to check the official websites or visitor centers of Yellowstone (*https://www.yellowstonepark.com/park/faqs/visitor-centers-yellowstone*) and Grand Teton National Parks (*https://www.nps.gov/grte/index.htm*) for the most up-to-date information on festivals, events, and programs. The parks may have additional events throughout the year that cater to various interests and provide unique experiences for visitors.

CHAPTER 10: EXPLORING YELLOWSTONE
AND GRANDTETON FOR CHILDREN

Visiting Yellowstone and Grand Teton National Parks can be a wonderful and educational experience for children. Here are some tips and activities to make the most of your family trip:

1. JUNIOR RANGER PROGRAM: Both Yellowstone and Grand Teton offer Junior Ranger programs designed to engage children in learning about the parks' natural and cultural resources. Children can pick up activity booklets at visitor centers, complete age-appropriate activities, and attend ranger-led programs to earn a Junior Ranger badge. | *2. WILDLIFE SPOTTING:* Children are often fascinated by wildlife. Help them spot animals like bison, elk, and moose while driving through the parks. Encourage them to keep a wildlife journal or take photos of the animals they see. | *3. GEOTHERMAL FEATURES:* The geothermal features in Yellowstone, such as geysers and hot springs, can captivate children's imagination. Take them to see Old Faithful erupt and explore the boardwalks around geothermal areas. Explain the science behind these natural wonders in an age-appropriate manner. | *4. HIKING AND NATURE TRAILS:* Both parks offer family-friendly hiking trails suitable for children. Look for shorter and easier trails, such as the Fairy Falls Trail in Yellowstone or the Hidden Falls and Inspiration Point Trail in Grand Teton.

Along the way, encourage children to observe and appreciate the surrounding nature. | *5. VISITOR CENTERS AND MUSEUMS:* Visit the visitor centers and museums within the parks. These facilities often have interactive exhibits and displays that can engage children in learning about the park's geology, wild life, and history. Encourage them to ask questions and participate in any hands-on activities available.

6. BOAT RIDES AND SCENIC DRIVES: Take a boat ride on Jenny Lake in Grand Teton or a scenic drive along the Teton Park Road. Children can enjoy the scenic views, learn about the park's features from interpretive signs, and spot wildlife from the comfort of the boat or car. | *7. PICNICS AND OUTDOOR PLAY:* Pack a picnic lunch and find a suitable spot to enjoy a meal amidst nature. Many picnic areas within the parks offer beautiful views and a chance for children to run around and play. Take advantage of these opportunities for outdoor play and exploration. | *8. STARGAZING AND NIGHTTIME ACTIVITIES:* Take advantage of the parks' dark skies for stargazing. Point out constellations and encourage children to make their own observations. Consider attending a ranger-led nighttime program to learn about nocturnal animals or listen to stories around a campfire.

9. WILDLIFE AND NATURE PHOTOGRAPHY: Encourage children to bring a camera or smartphone to capture their favorite moments and the beauty of nature. Teach them about composition and encourage them to document their experiences.

Keep safety as your top priority during your family vacation. Keep children close by, follow park regulations, and be aware of wildlife safety guidelines. Engaging children in hands-on experiences and encouraging their curiosity will foster a love for nature and create lasting memories of your visit to Yellowstone and Grand Teton National Parks.

CHAPTER 11: PRACTICAL INFORMATION

- *Packing List*
- *Shopping & Sourvenirs*
- *Safety Tips and Guidelines*
- *Useful Contacts*
- *Useful Resources*

PACKING LIST

When preparing for your trip to Yellowstone and Grand Teton National Parks, consider packing the following essentialsWhen packing for Yellowstone and Grand Teton National Parks, it's essential to be prepared for varying weather conditions and outdoor activities. Here's a comprehensive packing list:

1. CLOTHING

- Lightweight and breathable clothing (short-sleeved shirts, shorts, etc)
- Long-sleeved shirts and pants for sun and insect protection
- Warm layers (fleece or down jacket, thermal underwear) for cooler evenings
- Waterproof and windproof jacket
- Comfortable hiking boots or sturdy shoes
- Hat with a wide brim or baseball cap for sun protection
- Gloves or mittens (for early mornings or high elevations)

2. RAIN GEAR

- Waterproof rain jacket or poncho
- Waterproof pants or rainproof cover for pants

3. ACCESSORIES

- Sunglasses with UV protection
- Sunscreen with high SPF
- Insect repellent
- Reusable water bottle
- Daypack for hikes and day trips
- Binoculars for wildlife viewing
- Camera or smartphone for capturing memories

4. CAMPING EQUIPMENT (IF APPLICABLE)

- Tent with rainfly
- Sleeping bag suitable for the expected temperatures
- Sleeping pad or air mattress for added comfort
- Camping stove and cooking utensils

- Food and snacks (consider bear-proof containers if camping)

5. PERSONAL ITEMS

- Valid ID, driver's license, or passport
- Medical insurance cards
- Prescription medications
- Personal hygiene items (toothbrush, toothpaste, etc.)

6. MAPS AND GUIDES

- Maps and guidebooks of Yellowstone and Grand Teton National Parks

7. MISCELLANEOUS

- Cash or credit/debit cards (ATMs may not be widely available)
- Portable phone charger and charging cables
- Travel itinerary and reservation confirmations
- First aid kit with basic medical supplies
- Trash bags for waste disposal during hikes
- Travel towel or bandana
- Ziplock bags for organizing small items

*Always remember to check the weather forecast for your
travel dates and make appropriate plans accordingly.
Always be respectful of the parks' rules and regulations
and prioritize Leave No Trace principles to help protect
these natural wonders for future generations.*

SHOPPING & SOUVENIRS

When visiting Yellowstone and Grand Teton National Parks, You'll find a variety of shops and gift stores within Yellowstone and Grand Teton National Parks, as well as in nearby towns for shopping and purchasing souvenirs. Here are some popular options: *1. Visitor Centers:* Both parks have visitor centers with gift shops offering a wide range of souvenirs, including T-shirts, hats, mugs, magnets, postcards, and books about the parks' wildlife, geology, and history. | *2. General Stores:* Within the parks, there are general stores that sell a variety of essential items, snacks, and basic souvenirs. | *3. Gift Shops at Lodges:* Many lodges within and around the parks have gift shops where you can find unique items specific to the lodge and the parks. | *4. Local Art and Crafts:* Look for Native American craft shops or galleries that offer traditional arts and crafts made by local artisans, such as pottery, jewelry, and handmade textiles. | *5. Photography and Art Prints:* You can find stunning landscape photographs & art prints inspired by the beauty of the parks. | *6. Outdoor Gear:* Some gift shops may offer outdoor gear & equipment like water bottles, hiking sticks, and binoculars. | *7. Food and Beverages:* Local food products, such as huckleberry treats & other regional specialties, can be found in the park's gift shops. | *8. Ranger-Related Items:* Look for ranger-themed souvenirs like patches, badges & ranger hats.

Some popular souvenirs and items to consider include:

- T-shirts, hats, and apparel featuring park logos or wildlife designs
- Books and field guides about the parks' flora, fauna, and geology
- Local artwork and photography capturing the beauty of the parks
- Native American crafts and jewelry
- Huckleberry products, such as jams, syrups, and chocolates
- Bison-themed items, including mugs, keychains, and plush toys

SAFETY TIPS AND GUIDELINES

While visiting Yellowstone and Grand Teton National Parks, it's essential to prioritize safety and follow guidelines to ensure a safe and enjoyable experience. Here are some important safety tips to consider:

1. Stay on Designated Trails: Stick to marked trails and boardwalks to protect yourself and the delicate ecosystems. Venturing off can be dangerous and may harm sensitive natural features.

2. Wildlife Safety: Keep a safe distance (at least 25 yards/23 meters) from all wildlife and 100 yards/91 meters from bears and wolves. Use binoculars and telephoto lenses for closer views. Never feed or approach animals.

3. Beware of Thermal Features: Heed warning signs and stay away from hot springs, geysers, and thermal pools. The water is scalding and can cause severe burns.

4. Weather Awareness: Be prepared for sudden weather changes. Dress in layers and bring rain gear, as mountain weather can be unpredictable.

5. Altitude and Hydration: Both parks have high elevations, so stay hydrated by drinking plenty of water. Take it easy if you're not accustomed to higher altitudes to avoid altitude sickness.

6. Road Safety: Observe speed limits and wildlife crossings on roads. Exercise caution while driving, especially during dawn and dusk when animals are more active.

7. Carry Bear Spray: If hiking in bear country, carry bear spray and know how to use it. When hiking, ensure you travel in groups and make noise to alert bears of your presence.

8. Proper Food Storage: Store all food, trash, and scented items in bear-proof containers or lockers. This prevents attracting bears to your campsite.

9. Stay Informed: Check weather conditions, park alerts, and any safety advisories before heading out.

10. Cell Service and GPS: It's essential to have a physical map and know your route as well. GPS can sometimes be unreliable, especially in remote areas with limited cell service or no signal.

11. *Swimming Safety:* Swimming is only allowed in designated areas. Cold water temperatures and strong currents can be hazardous.

12. *Fire Safety:* Follow all fire regulations and guidelines. Extinguish campfires completely before leaving.

13. *Emergency Preparedness:* Know the location of emergency services, first aid stations, and contact information for park rangers.

14. *Leave No Trace:* Respect nature and wildlife by leaving no trace of your visit. Pack out all trash and minimize your impact on the environment.

By following these safety tips and guidelines, you can fully enjoy the natural wonders of Yellowstone and Grand Teton National Parks while helping to protect the parks for future generations.

USEFUL CONTACTS

USEFUL CONTACTS FOR YELLOWSTONE

YELLOWSTONE NATIONAL PARK HEADQUARTERS

Address: 100 Sylvan Pass Road, Mammoth Hot Springs, WY 82116 | *Phone:* (307) 344-7381 | *Website:* https://www.nps.gov/yell/

YELLOWSTONE NATIONAL PARK VISITOR CENTERS

Mammoth Hot Springs Visitor Center: *Address:* 120 Norris Road, Mammoth Hot Springs, WY 82116 | *Phone:* (307) 344-7301

Old Faithful Visitor Center: *Address:* 1 Old Faithful Inn Road, Upper Geyser Basin, WY 82190 | *Phone:* (307) 344-7301

Grant Village Visitor Center: *Address:* 1 Grand Loop Road, Grant Village, WY 82190 | *Phone:* (307) 344-7301

Yellowstone National Park Emergency Dispatch: *Phone:* (307) 344-2535

USEFUL CONTACTS FOR GRAND TETON NATIONAL PARK

Grand Teton National Park Headquarters: *Address:* 120 South Cache Street, Moose, WY 83012 | *Phone:* (307) 739-3300 | *Website:* https://www.nps.gov/grte

GRAND TETON NATIONAL PARK VISITOR CENTERS

Moose Visitor Center: *Address:* 120 South Cache Street, Moose, WY 83012 | *Phone:* (307) 739-3300

Jenny Lake Visitor Center: *Address:* 1000 South Jenny Lake Road, Moose, WY 83012 | *Phone:* (307) 739-3300

Colter Bay Visitor Center: *Address:* 200 Colter Bay Road, Colter Bay Village, WY 83013 | *Phone:* (307) 739-3300

Grand Teton National Park Emergency Dispatch: *Phone:* (307) 739-3300

USEFUL RESOURCES

1. National park Service (NPS) Official Website: *Yellowstone National Park: www.nps.gov/yell | Grand Teton National Park: www.nps.gov/grte*

2. Yellowstone National Park Official website: *www.yellowstonepark.com*

3. Yellowstone National Park Maps: *https://npmaps.com/yellowstone | https://npmaps.com/grand-teton*

4. Official Park Maps and Brochures: These can be obtained from visitor centers or downloaded from the NPS websites.

5. Local Visitor Centers and Ranger Stations: These facilities offer information, exhibits, and programs to enhance your park experience.

6. Park Apps and Online Resources: Download official park apps or visit the park websites for up-to-date information on park alerts, road conditions, and activities.

7. Guidebooks and Travel Websites: Look for guidebooks and reputable travel websites that provide detailed information on the parks, attractions, and activities.

By being prepared, informed, and following safety guidelines, you can ensure a smooth and enjoyable experience while exploring Yellowstone and Grand Teton National Parks.

MAP

Map 1: Old Faithful trail map showing the trails, boardwalks, geysers, and thermal features in the southeastern part of the Upper Geyser Basin, nearest Old Faithful Geyser.

Map 2: Old Faithful area trail map showing the northwest continuation of map 1, including Riverside Geyser, Giant Geyser, Morning Glory Pool, and the Biscuit Basin

Map 3: Norris Geyser Basin trail map, showing geysers and hot springs in both the Porcelain Basin and Back Basin

Map 4: Mammoth Hot Springs trail map showing the terraces, springs, trails, and boardwalks in the Mammoth Hot Springs area.

Map 5: West Thumb Geyser Basin trail map, showing the geysers and thermal features such as Fishing Cone on the west shore of Yellowstone Lake near Grant Village.

Map 6: Grand Canyon of the Yellowstone trail map showing the trails accessing both Upper and Lower Falls.

Map 7: Fountain Paint Pot trail map (50 kb), showing the trails surrounding the Fountain Paint Pots and thermal features in the Lower Geyser Basin, including popular Clepsydra Geyser

MAP 1: OLD FAITHFUL TRAIL MAP

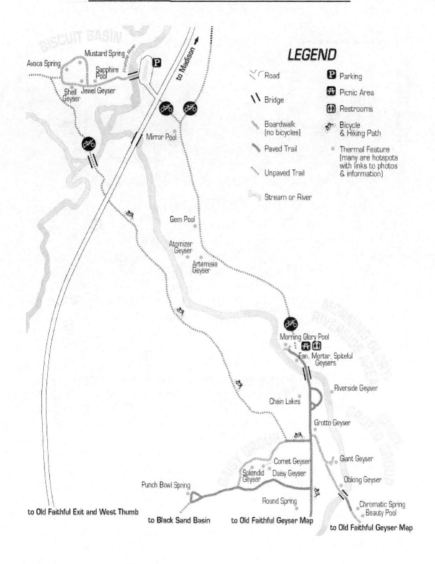

LEGEND

- ⚡ Road
- \\ Bridge
- Boardwalk (no bicycles)
- Paved Trail
- Unpaved Trail
- Stream or River
- 🅿 Parking
- 🏕 Picnic Area
- 🚻 Restrooms
- 🚲 Bicycle & Hiking Path
- • Thermal Feature (many are hotspots with links to photos & information)

BISCUIT BASIN

Avoca Spring
Mustard Spring
Sapphire Pool
Shell Geyser
Jewel Geyser
to Madison
Mirror Pool
Gem Pool
Atomizer Geyser
Artemisia Geyser
Morning Glory Pool
Fan, Mortar, Spiteful Geysers
Riverside Geyser
Chain Lakes
Grotto Geyser
Comet Geyser
Giant Geyser
Splendid Geyser
Daisy Geyser
Oblong Geyser
Punch Bowl Spring
Round Spring
Chromatic Spring
Beauty Pool

to Old Faithful Exit and West Thumb

to Black Sand Basin

to Old Faithful Geyser Map

to Old Faithful Geyser Map

213

MAP 2: OLD FAITHFUL AREA TRAIL MAP

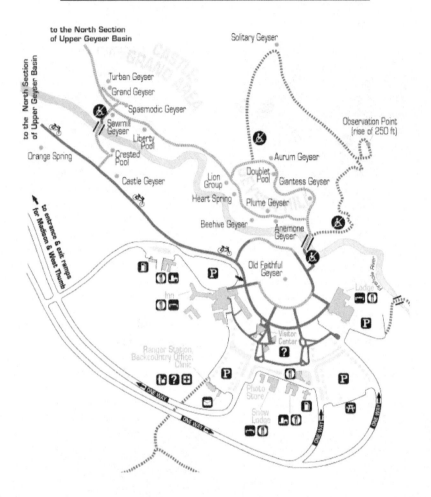

to the North Section
of Upper Geyser Basin

Solitary Geyser

to the North Section of Upper Geyser Basin

Turban Geyser

Grand Geyser

Spasmodic Geyser

Sewmill Geyser

Liberty Pool

Orange Spring

Crested Pool

Castle Geyser

Observation Point
(rise of 250 ft)

Aurum Geyser

Lion Group

Doublet Pool

Giantess Geyser

Heart Spring

Plume Geyser

Beehive Geyser

Anemone Geyser

Old Faithful Geyser

to entrance & exit ramps
for Madison & West Thumb

Inn

P

Visitor Center

Lodge

P

Ranger Station,
Backcountry Office,
Clinic

P

Photo Store

Snow Lodge

P

ONE WAY

ONE WAY

ONE WAY

ONE WAY

CASTLE GRAND AREA

Firehole River

MAP 3: NORRIS GEYSER
BASIN TRAIL MAP

North

Feet
0 ...... 330 660
0 ...... 100 200
Meters

Legend

▬▬▬ Dirt or paved trail
▪▪▪▪ Stairs, steep grades, or uneven ground
▬▬▬ Boardwalk
░░░ Road and Parking Area
● Hydrothermal feature
🅿 Parking

MAP 4: MAMMOTH HOT SPRINGS TRAIL MAP

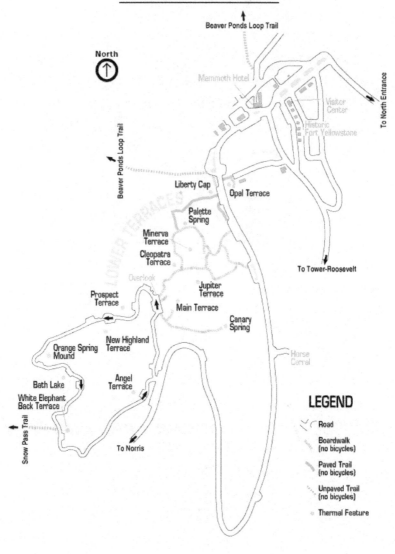

Beaver Ponds Loop Trail

North

Mammoth Hotel

Visitor Center

Historic Fort Yellowstone

To North Entrance

Beaver Ponds Loop Trail

Liberty Cap

Opal Terrace

Paletta Spring

Minerva Terrace

Cleopatra Terrace

LOWER TERRACES

Overlook

Jupiter Terrace

To Tower-Roosevelt

Prospect Terrace

Main Terrace

Canary Spring

Orange Spring Mound

New Highland Terrace

Horse Corral

Bath Lake

Angel Terrace

White Elephant Back Terrace

Snow Pass Trail

To Norris

LEGEND

- Road
- Boardwalk (no bicycles)
- Paved Trail (no bicycles)
- Unpaved Trail (no bicycles)
- Thermal Feature

MAP 5: WEST THUMB GEYSER
BASIN TRAIL MAP

MAP 6: GRAND CANYON OF THE YELLOWSTONE TRAIL MAP

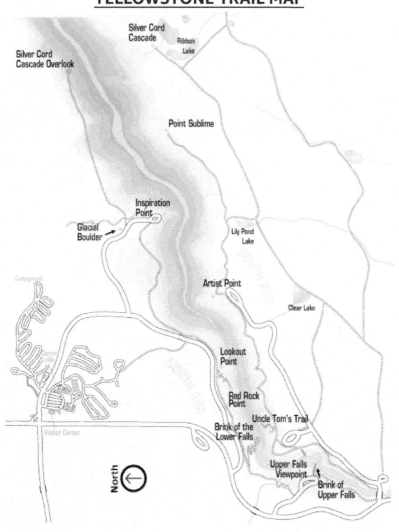

MAP 7: FOUNTAIN PAINT POT TRAIL MAP

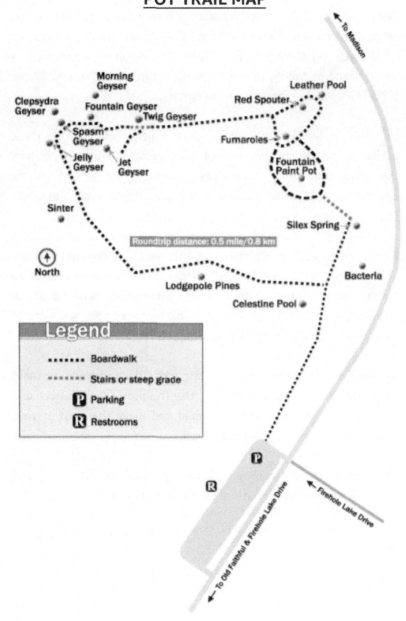

CONCLUSION

Yellowstone and Grand Teton National Parks offer incredible natural beauty, diverse wildlife, and a range of outdoor activities for visitors of all ages. Whether you're exploring the geothermal wonders of Yellowstone or taking in the majestic mountains of Grand Teton, there is something for everyone to enjoy.

In this guide, we covered various aspects of visiting these parks, including an overview of each park, planning your trip, top attractions, nearby excursions, itineraries, dining and lodging options, family-friendly activities, practical information, and safety tips.

From geysers and hot springs to wildlife watching and hiking trails, Yellowstone and Grand Teton National Parks provide a chance to connect with nature and create lifelong memories. Whether you're traveling with family, friends, or solo, the parks offer a wealth of experiences to suit your interests and preferences.

Remember to plan ahead, respect the park's rules and guidelines, and prioritize safety during your visit. Use the provided resources and contact information to stay informed and make the most of your time in these remarkable national parks.

Enjoy your journey through Yellowstone and Grand Teton, and immerse yourself in the natural wonders that await you!

OTHER BOOKS BY THIS AUTHOR

Scan the QR Code Above or Click the Link below to See
More books from this Author (All Books are Available
in Kindle, Paperback and Hardcover)

CLICK HERE TO SEE ALL BOOKS BY THIS AUTHOR

ABOUT THE AUTHOR

 Nicholas Ingram is a seasoned travel enthusiast and a passionate writer with a deep love for exploring new places and immersing in diverse cultures. With a wealth of experience spanning over 23 years, Nick has become a trusted voice in the world of travel writing. Nick embarked on his first solo adventure at the age of 21, and since then he hasn't looked back. Nick believes that travel is not just about visiting new destinations, but about forging connections with people, understanding their way of life, and embracing the beauty of our world. As a seasoned travel guide writer, Nick has authored more than 10 books and numerous articles on destinations around the globe. Nick is known for his ability to provide readers with comprehensive, practical, and inspiring insights into the places he cover. Nick doesn't just stop at guidebooks. He is a firm believer in sustainable travel and actively advocate for responsible tourism. His writings often emphasize the importance of respecting local communities and preserving the natural environment. When Nick isn't busy penning down travel guides, you can find him seeking out hidden gems, indulging in local cuisines, or engaging in meaningful conversations with fellow travelers. His curiosity knows no bounds, and he is always on the lookout for the next great adventure. | **WEBSITE:** https://www.amazon.com/stores/author/B0C2LVJY5W/about | https://www.amazon.com/author/nicholasingram | https://www.amazon.com/stores/author/B0C2LVJY5W/allbooks | **EMAIL:** *theworldexplorergs@gmail.com* | **X (FORMERLY TWITTER):** *@daworldexplorer*

YOUR FEEDBACK

Thank You So Much For Reading this Far!

I sincerely appreciate the time you've taken to read my book this far. As a small independent publisher, your support means a great deal, and I hope my guide is making a difference in your traveling journey. If you could spare just 60 seconds, I would love to hear your honest feedback on Amazon. Your reviews are incredibly valuable and help other travelers too. To leave your feedback, follow the steps below:

1. Open your camera app | 2. Scan the QR code below with your mobile device | 3. The review page will open in your web browser | 4. Write your review and submit.

OR ENTER THE URL BELOW IN YOUR BROWSER

https://tinyurl.com/yellgtnp

When the review page opens, Rate this guide with stars (one to five) based on your experience from reading/using this guide. | Write a review in the provided text box. | Proofread and submit. | Allow a few days for your review to appear.

Thank you so much!

Made in the USA
Coppell, TX
25 June 2024

33931895R00134